Laura Wright
English Grammar for Literature Students

Laura Wright

English Grammar for Literature Students

How to Analyse Literary Texts

ISBN 978-3-11-134841-4
e-ISBN (PDF) 978-3-11-134889-6

Library of Congress Control Number: 2024935214

Bibliographic information published by the Deutsche Nationalbibliothek
The Deutsche Nationalbibliothek lists this publication in the Deutsche Nationalbibliografie;
detailed bibliographic data are available on the internet at http://dnb.dnb.de.

© 2024 Walter de Gruyter GmbH, Berlin/Boston
Cover image: gonin / iStock / Getty Images Plus
Typesetting: Integra Software Services Pvt. Ltd

www.degruyter.com

Acknowledgements

Thanks are due to the Faculty of English, University of Cambridge; to Prof Jonathan Culpeper, University of Lancaster, Prof Bas Aarts, University College London, and Prof Louise Sylvester, University of Westminster, for reviewing drafts; and to Pedram Badakhchani of the Language Centre, University of Cambridge, for designing the clause diagrams.

Contents

Chapter	Literary Author	Pages
Acknowledgements		V
Introduction		1
1 On Nouns	Seamus Heaney, W. H. Auden	5
2 Premodification in the Noun Phrase	Kingsley Amis, Dylan Thomas	13
3 On Adjectives	Ben Okri, Zelda Fitzgerald	21
4 On Definite and Indefinite Articles	Arthur Morrison, Graham Greene	29
5 Personal Pronouns	A. C. Jacobs, Derek Walcott	35
6 Prepositional Phrases	John Betjeman, H. G. Wells	43
7 On Verbs: Tense	Jeanette Winterson, Harold Pinter	49
8 Phrasal Verbs	James Joyce, Philip Larkin	57
9 Auxiliary Verbs	Denton Welch, Elizabeth Taylor	63
10 Auxiliary Verb *do*	Laurie Graham, Jerome K. Jerome	71
11 Modal Auxiliary Verbs	Penelope Fitzgerald, David Mamet	77
12 On Aspect	F. Tennyson Jesse, Raymond Chandler	87
13 Adverbs	John Dryden, Mary Robinson	95
14 Adverbials	Edwige Danticat, Henry Green, F. Scott Fitzgerald	105
15 On Clauses	Jean Rhys, Jack Kerouak	117

16	**On Clauses: Coordinators and Subordinators**	Ogden Nash, Mervyn Peake	**125**
17	**On Clauses: Relative Pronouns**	Lee A. Tonouchi, Ian Duhig	**131**
18	***-ing* forms**	Sam Selvon, Anita Brookner	**141**
19	**On Anaphora**	C. B. Poultney, M. G. Sanchez	**149**
20	**On Cataphora**	Graham Swift, Virginia Woolf	**153**
21	**End Focus and Endweight**	Stevie Smith, Stevie Smith	**159**
22	**Collocation and Colligation**	E. M. Forster, Evelyn Waugh	**167**
23	**Cohesion and Coherence**	Muriel Spark, Caryl Churchill	**173**
24	**Deixis**	Thom Gunn, Elizabeth Bishop	**181**
25	**Conversational Implicatures**	Stevie Smith, Kingsley Amis, Nell Dunn	**191**
26	**Speech Acts**	M. J. Farrell (Molly Keane), Tama Janowicz	**199**

Primary Sources — **205**

References — **207**

Index — **209**

Introduction

People study literature for many reasons. In these pages you will read extracts from fiction written in Chicago English, Californian English, Gibraltarian English, Hawai'ian English, Irish English, London English, Midlands English, Trinidadian English, Welsh English – stories set in places you may never have been to, written in dialects you may never have seen before, or long before you were born. Literature is an emotional rollercoaster as characters fall in love, die, betray, argue, kill. Literature widens the world, showing us what it's like to be a Victorian pauper or a murdering queen or a twentieth-century estate agent. Empathising with the protagonist, girls become boys and boys become girls. Literature puzzles – did the governess really see ghosts in *The Turn of the Screw*? Did Hamlet? Literature teaches – we learn from Robinson Crusoe how to load cargo onto a raft so that it won't fall off when navigating between shoals in a strong ocean current, and from Huckleberry Finn how to capture a raft careering midstream in thick fog at night on the Mississippi River. The first was published in 1719, the second in 1884, but the behaviour of rafts in strong currents hasn't changed.

Literature does all these things and more by authors choosing words and putting them in order. By learning about how English works, you will begin to see how literature has the effect it does – how it is that you are moved to tears, or startled into laughing out loud, or flummoxed by a diversionary tactic so that you don't notice a plot point, causing surprise at the denouement like a conjuring trick. You will see how authors convey such universal states as boredom, suspense, fear, worry, evasion, double-edged bitchiness; or the simultaneous experience of contradictory emotions. Ambiguity on the page is the author's friend and there are many ways of saying things so that meaning cannot be decided one way or the other. Indeed Chapters 9, 10 and 11 are a little manual on how to lie successfully – use passives without a *by*-agent to suppress who did what, auxiliary verb *do* to cover up whatever it was you did, and deontic and epistemic modals to mislead and divert. A post split-up text by Anita Brookner in Chapter 18 shows the agentless potential of nonfinite *-ing*, useful for conveying nonfactual fantasy: another trick worth bearing in mind if you want to improve your lying skills.

But you might be interested in language for its own sake, and you can use this book as an entertaining way of learning about grammar and discourse pragmatics. For example, the concept known in linguistics as *anaphoric reference* is currently defined in Wikipedia as "the use of an expression that depends specifically upon an antecedent expression and thus is contrasted with cataphora, which is the use of an expression that depends upon a postcedent expression. The anaphoric (referring term is called an anaphor" and there's nothing wrong with that,[1] but readers may find it easier to learn about anaphor via M. G. Sanchez's bilingual text in chapter 19 on page 150 about a penis.

I pause here, as I know you have now turned to page 150 to read about the penis.

To resume, humour is a great aid to learning. Lee A. Tonouchi's text on page 133 exemplifies interrogative pronouns far more concisely than any grammar-book and in a manner which all air passengers can relate to: "dis flight attendant stewardess-man is jus one rude dude, cuss. Ees like he tink I looking him wot, so he looking me why, only I not looking him wot, I looking him, I THIRSTY WEA MY DRINK, cuss". Ogden Nash's verse on page 126 exemplifies clause coordinators: "But Ferdinand said America was a bird in the bush and he'd rather have a berdinand". If you enjoy reading wit, you may enjoy learning how that wit functions.

Alternatively you might want to learn how to write effectively. Chapter 12 analyses a text by Raymond Chandler to show the effect of restricting aspect to simple auxiliary-less verbs, in order to mirror the observation-process of a detective who lacks knowledge about events and has to make deductions from what he observes in front of him. This omission of auxiliary verbs has been much copied by subsequent writers of detective fiction, and we can all learn from a master. A poem by Stevie Smith demonstrates the effect of too much information in the rebuttal of a marriage proposal (which is never going to be an easy linguistic ask) in her short poem *Lady 'Rogue' Singleton* on page 191. She is mistress of the strategic placement – at the end of a poem on page 191, in the middle of one on page 162. But it is not just writing well that literature teaches: speaking skills can be improved too by analysing how characters talk on the page. Phaetic communication is the linguistic term for what is commonly known as 'small talk', that semantically empty but socially obligatory discourse we perform every time we meet someone we know, which some people never really learn how to do and are thus regarded as unfriendly, whereas others learn it early and are regarded as charming. In a text by Kingsley Amis on page 193 two people who were briefly a couple in their youth meet up again in old age, with attendant awkwardness. Amis shows what not to do and what not to say when in such a situation – and men, what not to wear.

Each chapter follows the same structure, with a short introduction to the linguistic feature in question, a demonstration of that feature in a literary extract, followed by an opportunity for the reader to spot the feature in a subsequent literary extract, and a discussion of the effect. Linguistic explanations are kept to a

---

[1] https://en.wikipedia.org/wiki/Anaphora_(linguistics), accessed 15/06/2023.

minimum so that the literary authors take centre stage for maximum enjoyment; likewise, footnotes and references are deliberately few.

Finally, please don't worry if you find grammatical analysis hard. Linguists also find it hard as we don't yet fully understand how grammar works. A whole PhD thesis has been written on possible ways of analysing the grammar of Philip Larkin's short poem *Mr Bleaney* on page 59.[2] On page 108–9 the extract from a novel by Henry Green is so complex that it can be analysed in more ways than I have space to explain. Linguists find this kind of thing exhilarating – there are still new models of grammar to be created, and new linguistic discoveries to be made. If you don't understand something, it may be because we haven't grasped it yet, and you may go on to be the person who finds the solution.

---

[2] Cauldwell, R.T. (1994) 'Discourse Intonation and Recordings of Poetry: Philip Larkin Reads *Mr Bleaney*', unpublished doctoral dissertation, University of Birmingham.

1 On Nouns

1 Definition of term *noun*

You might have learnt that a noun is a 'naming' word. This is true – names of people and places are nouns: *Boadicea, The Minch, The Pillars of Hercules*; and so are the names of things: *eye, paw, loris, fruit*. However, working with this definition will send you adrift when you confront individual texts: *The large-eyed loris paws the fruit*. Or, *The small-pawed loris eyes the fruit*. In these sentences, only *loris* and *fruit* are nouns (adjectives *large-eyed, small-pawed* and verbs *paws, eyes* will be dealt with in later chapters). Also, it is a less helpful concept when dealing with intangibles like *frisson, creep, telekinesis*. Nouns are far more easily identified by the way in which they fit into phrases. If the word in context can sit in the testframe

    the/a/an _____

then it's usually a noun:

The loris	*a* frisson
A paw	*a* creep
An eye	*the* telekinesis

Almost all nouns take an *–s* in the plural and apostrophe *–'s* in possessive groups: *the* lorises, *the* loris's *paw*.

Names of people, places, entities, dates and times are known as Proper Nouns and by convention they are capitalised:

Queen Victoria
Christmas Day
Google
Tuesday
Mid-Atlantic Ridge

Compound nouns consist of two words which may or may not be nouns themselves: blackboard, bus shelter, go-between (test: *the blackboard, a bus shelter, the go-between*). Three word compounds do occur but are far less frequent: hug-me-tight (a dancer's cross-over cardigan), forget-me-not (a flower), father-in-law. Typographically compound nouns can take a hyphen, a white space, or be written all as one word. The choice is to a large extent decided by each publishing house's house-style, and how it looks to the writer on the page (I didn't write housestyle as it doesn't immediately look divisible, but I could have written house style). Notice how some compound nouns can have a colloquial flavour:

> pull-ons, pullovers, roll-ons, step-ins, pop-overs

These were all types of twentieth-century female clothing. *Pull-ons, roll-ons* and *step-ins* were types of girdle to flatten the stomach, and a *pop-over* was a tunic worn over a jumper and tights. These particular compound nouns consist of [verb + preposition], and semantically they indicate how the garment is put on. *Make-up* and *cross-over* (a type of nineteenth-century shawl) also fit the pattern, as does *pinafore* (and *drawers*, an old-fashioned word for pants or knickers, follows the same semantic path). The reason for the colloquial flavour is because many nouns consisting of [verb + preposition] are relatively new in the system. Contrast *dandelion*, which is an older, three-component compound, Anglo-Norman French *dent de lion* 'tooth of lion'.

2 Demonstration of term *noun*

Compound nouns used to be a crucial constituent of Old English poetry. Here is a modern poem composed with the Old English tradition in mind. I have marked common nouns in maroon, compound nouns in green, and Proper Nouns in orange:

> Dogger, Rockall, Malin, Irish Sea:
> Green, swift upsurges, North Atlantic flux
> Conjured by that strong gale-warning voice
> Collapse into a sibilant penumbra.
> Midnight and closedown. Sirens of the tundra,
> Of eel-road, seal-road, keel-road, whale-road, raise
> Their wind-compounded keen behind the baize
> And drive the trawlers to the lee of Wicklow.
> L'Etoile, Le Guillemot, La Belle Hélène
> Nursed their bright names this morning in the bay
> That toiled like mortar. It was marvelous
> And actual, I said out loud, 'A haven,'
> The word deepening, clearing, like the sky
> Elsewhere on Minches, Cromarty, The Faroes.
>
> Seamus Heaney, 1979, from *Glanmore Sonnets*, VII

I have not marked *North Atlantic, gale-warning*, or *wind-compounded*, because in context they are not acting as nouns but as compound adjectives modifying the noun to their right: *North Atlantic flux, strong gale-warning voice, wind-compounded keen* (more on noun premodifiers in chapter 4).

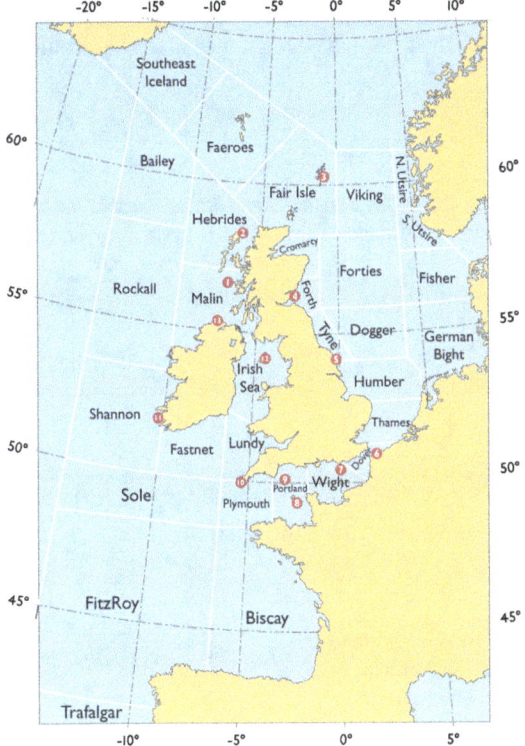

Map of Sea Areas and Coastal Weather Stations referred to in the Shipping Forecast.
https://en.wikipedia.org/wiki/Shipping_Forecast.

Eel-road, seal-road, keel-road, whale-road are a type of Old English compound known as a *kenning*. A kenning is a poetical device used in Old Icelandic and Old English poetry using two words to express a concept imaginatively. In this case, all four compounds are different ways of expressing the concept *sea*. Although this sonnet is about a sea gale reported by the Shipping Forecast on the radio before the station closes down for the night, the nouns evoke places: the names of the North Atlantic sea areas, Ireland, the sheltering fishing-boats from Northern France, and the mythology of Old English poetry. Because of the waves of settlement by peoples speaking different languages these nouns are multilingual: English, French, Irish Gaelic (*Malin*), Scottish Gaelic (*Cromarty*), Old Icelandic (*The Faroes*, from *fær* 'sheep' + *ey* 'island'), possibly Old Norse (*Wicklow*), possibly Middle Dutch (*dogger* 'kind of fishing boat') – and also transferred from one to another. *Minch*, the name of the channel between the Hebrides and the Scottish mainland is likely to be French *manche*, 'sleeve', as French seafarers called the part of the North Sea between East Anglia and Holland *La Manche de l'Est* 'the eastern sleeve', and the part of the North Sea between Ireland and England *La Manche de l'Ouest*, 'the western sleeve'. The gales have blown the languages around.

References

Stiubhart, Domhnall Uilleam. 2017. The Making of the Minch: French Pirates, British Herring, and Vernacular Knowledges at an Eighteenth-Century Maritime Crossroads. In David Worthington (ed.), *The New Coastal History: Cultural and Environmental Perspectives from Scotland and Beyond*, 131–148. Cham, Switzerland: Palgrave Macmillan.
Oxford English Dictionary. www.oed.com: dogger, *n*.

3 Literary Exercise

Here is another storm-poem that shows consciousness of the old poetic form with compound nouns. Identify the nouns – what is their function?

First Things First

Woken, I lay in the arms of my own warmth and listened
To a storm enjoying its storminess in the winter dark
Till my ear, as it can when half-asleep or half-sober,
Set to work to unscramble that interjectory uproar,
Construing its airy vowels and watery consonants
Into a love-speech indicative of a Proper Name.

Scarcely the tongue I should have chosen, yet, as well
As harshness and clumsiness would allow, it spoke in your praise,
Kenning you a god-child of the Moon and the West Wind
With power to tame both real and imaginary monsters,
Likening your poise of being to an upland county,
Here green on purpose, there pure blue for luck.

Loud though it was, alone as it certainly found me,
It reconstructed a day of peculiar silence
When a sneeze could be heard a mile off, and had me walking
On a headland of lava beside you, the occasion as ageless
As the stare of any rose, your presence exactly
So once, so valuable, so very now.

This, moreover, at an hour when only too often
A smirking devil annoys me in beautiful English,

Predicting a world where every sacred location
Is a sand-buried site all cultured Texans do,
Misinformed and thoroughly fleeced by their guides,
And gentle hearts are extinct like Hegelian Bishops.

Grateful, I slept till a morning that would not say
How much it believed of what I said the storm had said
But quietly drew my attention to what had been done
—So many cubic metres the more in my cistern
Against a leonine summer—, putting first things first:
Thousands have lived without love, not one without water.

W. H. Auden, 1956, *First Things First*

Analysis

Here is the poem again, with common nouns in maroon, compound nouns in green, and Proper Nouns in orange:

Woken, I lay in the arms of my own warmth and listened
To a storm enjoying its storminess in the winter dark
Till my ear, as it can when half-asleep or half-sober,
Set to work to unscramble that interjectory uproar,
Construing its airy vowels and watery consonants
Into a love-speech indicative of a Proper Name.

Scarcely the tongue I should have chosen, yet, as well
As harshness and clumsiness would allow, it spoke in your praise,
Kenning you a god-child of the Moon and the West Wind
With power to tame both real and imaginary monsters,
Likening your poise of being to an upland county,
Here green on purpose, there pure blue for luck.

Loud though it was, alone as it certainly found me,
It reconstructed a day of peculiar silence
When a sneeze could be heard a mile off, and had me walking
On a headland of lava beside you, the occasion as ageless
As the stare of any rose, your presence exactly
So once, so valuable, so very now.

This, moreover, at an hour when only too often
A smirking devil annoys me in beautiful English,
Predicting a world where every sacred location
Is a sand-buried site all cultured Texans do,
Misinformed and thoroughly fleeced by their guides,
And gentle hearts are extinct like Hegelian Bishops.

> Grateful, I slept till a morning that would not say
> How much it believed of what I said the storm had said
> But quietly drew my attention to what had been done
> —So many cubic metres the more in my cistern
> Against a leonine summer—, putting first things first:
> Thousands have lived without love, not one without water.

In Stanza Two, I have marked *being* as a noun, because in context, it could be replaced by nouns such as *composure* or *comportment*, but *–ing* forms can be rather hard to classify: the *–ing* form in *paid for the writing of a poem* is preceded by an article (*the*), but the *–ing* form in *paid for writing a poem* could not easily take *the* or *a*, even though the meaning is the same. These types of *–ing* forms are known as *verbal nouns* (Chapter 18 is on *–ing* forms).

On purpose is a prepositional phrase, where the noun *purpose* is governed by the preposition *on*. Originally, the phrase was 'on set purpose'.

I have coloured the nouns that Auden capitalized as Proper Nouns, but this is his artistic judgement – in most modern texts, *bishop*, *moon* and *west wind* would not be so regarded. *Texans* would, being derived from a placename, and the philosopher Hegel was a person, hence the capital letter, but here *Hegelian* is used adjectivally, modifying the noun *bishop*. (By convention, capital letters are given to the compounds Proper Noun, Noun Phrase, Verb Phrase.)

Careful with *the more* in the last stanza (*So many cubic metres the more in my cistern*). The article *the* in front of it makes it look like a noun, but it is a comparative adjective: 'so many more cubic meters' (Chapter 3 is on adjectives).

The nouns can be sorted into semantic groups:

> *arms, ear, tongue, hearts*
> *vowels, consonants, tongue, love-speech, praise*
> *poise, being, presence, attention*
> *devil, monsters*
> *storm, moon, west wind, water*
> *day, occasion, hour, morning, summer*
> *county, headland, site, world, location*
> *cistern, metres, water*

Some of these nouns occur in the lexicon of Old English poetry (*west wind, moon*), or evoke Old English kennings: *love-speech*. Others evoke the mythological past (*devil, monsters*) and the geological past (*headland, lava*) versus the present age (*sneeze, cistern*). Three nouns take the suffix *–ness*: *storminess, harshness, clumsiness*. *–ness*, an Old English suffix, creates nouns from adjectives. *The Oxford English Dictionary* has some adroit examples of compounds under the headword -ness, *suffix*:

> 1859 G. A. Sala *Gaslight & Daylight* iv. 43 An irreproachable state of clean-shirtedness, navy blue-broadclothedness and chimney-pot-hattedness.

> 1901 *Academy* 8 June 495/2 Southport, with its sponge-cakeyness and schoolgirlism is surely worth study.

> 1949 P. Grainger *Let.* 23 Nov. in *All-round Man* (1994) 240 You are a love-child moving towards art. I am an artist moving towards love-child-ness.

Commentary

The poem is about the noise of a storm waking the narrator and sounding like the name of someone he is or was in love with who is no longer present. The morning reveals rainwater in the narrator's cistern, and he reflects in a practical way that living without love won't kill him. The nouns don't describe the storm, or the agonies of lost love. They are about more about concrete things: the narrator's present and his immediate future, not his past. He is moving on.

4 Teaching Point

Nouns are an important part of writing and most authors use lots of them. There are various suffixes (*-ness, -ism*) which form nouns, but the quickest means of identification is to use the testframe [*the* _____]. The ways in which nouns are used in literary writing has changed over time, and the Old English tradition of compounding no longer predominates. Looking up their etymologies and sorting them into semantic groups can quickly reveal affinities.

2 Premodification in the Noun Phrase

1 Definition of term *Premodification in the Noun Phrase*

Despite its long title this is a very useful and simple stylistic technique, and one that is easy to identify. You will recall from Chapter 1 that a noun is something that can be preceded meaningfully in context by *a/an* or *the*: a house, a kangaroo, the kettle. I say meaningfully in context because it's possible to use the same words in different grammatical contexts: 'wainscots house cockroaches', 'he kangarooed the fence', 'the police kettle the demonstrators' – where the same words are used as verbs. Therefore, if you look up *house* in a dictionary you'll find it listed as both a noun and a verb. So the test for a noun is: can it be preceded by *a/an* or *the* in context.

> 'Queens Park Rangers are on the up' – *up* is a noun in this context.
>
> 'We're going into the wide beyond' – *beyond* is a noun in this context.
>
> 'The *into* in this sentence has been nounified' – *into* is a noun in this context.

The whole thing, [*a/an* or *the* + noun], is called a Noun Phrase. It is normal to use light noun phrases like this, but it is also common to put modifying words, phrases or clauses in between the *a/an* or *the* [which are called *articles*] and the noun. Such inserted material modifies the meaning of the noun: 'a large house', 'a tremendously palace-like house', 'a very hard to run due to its size house'. However insertions like this aren't obligatory – a literary text could be written without any premodification in the Noun Phrase – so if an author puts premodified Noun Phrases into their text, it begs the question, why? What kind of information is being given? Different authors do very different things with this premodifying slot.

2 Demonstration of *Premodification in the Noun Phrase*

Read the following text, watching out for the nouns. Remember the test is: can you put *a/an* or *the* in front of the word you suspect might be a noun, in the context of the surrounding text?

A series of semi-intelligible pronouncements began by way of a microphone and one or two loudspeakers. As it proceeded the man Pugh, who now struck Charlie as distinctly deranged, kept sending him purposeful glances, promising him more to come, more to be communicated than just what he was called. Across the way, near the shape under the cloth, a smartly dressed youth who had to be the mayor introduced the, or merely a, minister of state at the Welsh Office. This man, who seemed scarcely older, spoke some formula and jerked at the end of an ornamental rope or cord that Charlie had not noticed before. With wonderful smoothness the red cloth parted and fell to reveal, standing on a plinth of what looked like olive-green marble, a shape in glossy yellow metal that was about the height of a human being without looking much more like one than the beaten-up chunk of stone that had stood there before.

There was a silence that probably came less from horror than sheer bafflement, then a sudden rush of applause. The presumed sculptor, a little fellow covered in hair like an artist in a cartoon, appeared and was the centre of attention for a few seconds. Another youngster, who said he represented the Welsh Arts Council, started talking about money. It came on to rain, though not enough to bother a Welsh crowd. On a second glance, the object on the plinth did look a certain amount like a man, but the style ruled out anything in the way of portraiture, and Charlie felt he was probably not the only one to wonder whether some handy abstraction – the spirit of Wales, say – had pushed out the advertised subject. Those close enough, however, could see Brydan's name on the plate along with just his dates, 1913–1960.

Alun's turn came. He played it low-key, avoiding a display of emotion so long after the event, sticking to facts, facts like Brydan being the greatest Welsh poet that had ever lived and also the greatest poet in the English language to have lived in the present century, together with minor but no less certain facts like his utter dedication to his art, though leaving out other ones like his utter dedication to Jack Daniel's Tennessee whiskey and *Astounding Science Fiction.*

Kingsley Amis, 1986, *The Old Devils*

The first task is to identify the nouns. In the text below, nouns are marked in red, with premodifiers in blue. I have put names – Proper Nouns – in orange, unless they occur in premodifying position. I have not coloured the pro-form *one* (which stands for nouns). Premodifying quantifiers (*few, some*) and enumerators (numbers) are given in green:

A series of semi-intelligible pronouncements began by way of a microphone and one or two loudspeakers. As it proceeded the man Pugh, who now struck Charlie as distinctly deranged, kept sending him purposeful glances, promising him more to come, more to be communicated than just what he was called. Across the way, near the shape under the cloth, a smartly dressed youth who had to be the mayor introduced the, or merely a, minister of state at the Welsh Office. This man, who seemed scarcely older, spoke some formula and jerked at the end of an ornamental rope or cord that Charlie had not noticed before. With wonderful smoothness the red cloth parted and fell to reveal, standing on a plinth of what looked like olive-green marble, a shape in glossy yellow metal that was about the height of a human being without looking much more like one than the beaten-up chunk of stone that had stood there before.

There was a silence that probably came less from horror than sheer bafflement, then a sudden rush of applause. The presumed sculptor, a little fellow covered in hair like an artist in a cartoon, appeared and was the centre of attention for a few seconds. Another youngster, who said he represented the Welsh Arts Council, started talking about money. It came on to rain, though not enough to bother a Welsh crowd. On a second glance, the object on the plinth did look a certain amount like a man, but the style ruled out anything in the way of portraiture, and Charlie felt he was probably not the only one to wonder whether some handy abstraction – the spirit of Wales, say – had pushed out the advertised subject. Those close enough, however, could see Brydan's name on the plate along with just his dates, 1913–1960.

Alun's turn came. He played it low-key, avoiding a display of emotion so long after the event, sticking to facts, facts like Brydan being the greatest Welsh poet that had ever lived and also the greatest poet in the English language to have lived in the present century, together with minor but no less certain facts like his utter dedication to his art, though leaving out other ones like his utter dedication to Jack Daniel's Tennessee whiskey and *Astounding Science Fiction*.

I have not highlighted *way* in *by way of* as the three words act as a single prepositional phrase, nor have I highlighted pro-forms – words which stand in for nouns – in the phrases '*more* (i.e. things) to come, *more* (i.e. things) to be communicated'; 'without looking much more like *one*' (i.e. a human), 'the only *one*' (i.e. person), 'other *ones*' (i.e. facts). You might have analysed Welsh Office and Welsh Arts Council as Welsh Office and Welsh Arts Council; I have analysed them as names due to their capitalisation, but left Jack Daniel's Tennessee whiskey as a Noun Phrase because Amis didn't capitalise *whiskey*.

Now that we've identified the Noun Phrases, our next task is to see what kind of information is given in the premodifying position. I select in particular:

semi-intelligible pronouncements
one or two loudspeakers
the, or merely a minister ('the, or merely a', premodifies 'minister', even though *or* means one or the other)
some formula
what looked like olive green marble
presumed sculptor
minor but no less certain facts

The modifiers serve to undercut the nouns. Not 'a sculptor', but 'a presumed sculptor'. Not 'olive green marble', but 'what looked like olive green marble'. We can find reinforcing lack of specificity or lack of certainty elsewhere in the text: a youth 'who had to be the mayor' rather than 'the mayor', 'an ornamental rope or cord' rather than 'an ornamental rope', a 'youngster who said he represented the Welsh Arts Council' rather than 'a youngster from the Welsh Arts Council'. Why might this be?

The extract is about Charlie watching the formal and ceremonial unveiling of a statue of the great Welsh poet, Brydan, who lived from 1913–1960. Alun gives a short eulogy. He proclaims what are twice said to be facts: that Brydan was 'the greatest Welsh poet that had ever lived and also the greatest poet in the English language to have lived in the present century'. He does not proclaim two undercutting facts: that the great Brydan was also an alcoholic and a low-brow science-fiction devotee.

Was Brydan a great literary figure or not? Does he merit the statue? In the context of the novel it is left unresolved, and the novel's central theme is about how to distinguish that which is genuine from that which is sham.

3 Literary Exercise

Identify the premodifiers in the following extract. What might be their function?

> [Silence]
>
> First Voice (*Very softly*)
>
> To begin at the beginning:
>
> It is spring, moonless night in the small town, starless and bible-black, the cobblestreets silent and the hunched, courters'-and-rabbits' wood limping invisible down to the sloeblack, slow, black, crowblack, fishingboat-bobbing sea.
>
> The houses are blind as moles (though moles see fine to-night in the snouting, velvet dingles) or blind as Captain Cat there in the muffled middle by the pump and the town clock, the shops in mourning, the Welfare Hall in widows' weeds. And all the people of the lulled and dumbfound town are sleeping now.
>
> Hush, the babies are sleeping, the farmers, the fishers, the tradesmen and pensioners, cobbler, school-teacher, postman and publican, the undertaker and the fancy woman, drunkard, dressmaker, preacher, policeman, the webfoot cocklewomen and the tidy wives. Young girls lie bedded soft or glide in their dreams, with rings and trousseaux, bridesmaided by glow-worms down the aisles of the

organplaying wood. The boys are dreaming wicked or of the bucking ranches of the night and the jollyrodgered sea. And the anthracite statues of the horses sleep in the fields, and the cows in the byres, and the dogs in the wetnosed yards; and the cats nap in the slant corners or lope sly, streaking and needling, on the one cloud of the roofs.

You can hear the dew falling, and the hushed town breathing. Only *your* eyes are unclosed to see the black and folded town fast, and slow, asleep. And you alone can hear the invisible starfall, the darkest-before-dawn minutely dew-grazed stir of the black, dab-filled sea where the *Arethusa*, the *Curlew* and the *Skylark*, *Zanzibar*, *Rhiannon*, the *Rover*, the *Cormorant*, and the *Star of Wales* tilt and ride.

Listen. It is night moving in the streets, the processional salt slow musical wind in Coronation Street and Cockle Row, it is the grass growing on Llareggub Hill, dewfall, starfall, the sleep of birds in Milk Wood.

Dylan Thomas, 1954, *Under Milk Wood, A Play for Voices*

Analysis

Here are the nouns in red, with their premodification in blue, and Proper Nouns (names) in orange. Premodifying enumerators are in green:

[Silence]

First Voice (*Very softly*)

To begin at the beginning:

It is spring, moonless night in the small town, starless and bible-black, the cobblestreets silent and the hunched, courters'-and-rabbits' wood limping invisible down to the sloeblack, slow, black, crowblack, fishingboat-bobbing sea.

The houses are blind as moles (though moles see fine to-night in the snouting, velvet dingles) or blind as Captain Cat there in the muffled middle by the pump and the town clock, the shops in mourning, the Welfare Hall in widows' weeds. And all the people of the lulled and dumbfound town are sleeping now.

Hush, the babies are sleeping, the farmers, the fishers, the tradesmen and pensioners, cobbler, school-teacher, postman and publican, the undertaker and the fancy woman, drunkard, dressmaker, preacher, policeman, the webfoot cocklewomen and the tidy wives. Young girls lie bedded soft or glide in their dreams, with rings and trousseaux, bridesmaided by glow-worms down the aisles of the organplaying wood. The boys are dreaming wicked or of the bucking ranches of the night and the jollyrodgered sea. And the anthracite statues of the horses sleep in the fields, and the cows in the byres, and the dogs in the wetnosed yards; and the cats nap in the slant corners or lope sly, streaking and needling, on the one cloud of the roofs.

You can hear the dew falling, and the hushed town breathing. Only *your* eyes are unclosed to see the black and folded town fast, and slow, asleep. And you alone can hear the invisible starfall, the darkest-before-dawn minutely dew-grazed stir of the black, dab-filled sea where the *Arethusa*, the *Curlew* and the *Skylark*, *Zanzibar*, *Rhiannon*, the *Rover*, the *Cormorant*, and the *Star of Wales* tilt and ride.

Listen. It is night moving in the streets, the processional salt slow musical wind in Coronation Street and Cockle Row, it is the grass growing on Llareggub Hill, dewfall, starfall, the sleep of birds in Milk Wood.

As Thomas sometimes puts hyphens in compound words and sometimes not, I have treated the first element of compound nouns as a modifier, unless the word is in common use (i.e. *tradesmen, school-teacher, undertaker, dressmaker*). I have treated *glow-worm* as a noun, rather than a premodifier and a noun, because it refers to a specific animal. But you might want to include all the first elements of the compound nouns in your analysis for the sake of consistency and you would be right to do so, in which case the premodifying count will be even higher. It's simply a question of convention – the convention has evolved of writing the compounds *undertaker, dressmaker* as though they were one word; *school-teacher, glow-worm* as though they were nearly one word or on the way to becoming one word, but not *jollyrodgered, organplaying, wetnosed* – these are Thomas' own.

Not only does Thomas put more words before nouns than is usual in speech, he also puts words in the premodifier position that don't usually sit in that position. In the following Noun Phrases the premodifiers do not usually collocate with the nouns [*Collocation* refers to the company words usually keep. *Addled* collocates with brains or eggs. *Rancid* collocates with oil, butter or bacon. *Tidy* collocates with a feature that can also be untidy – room, desk, moustache.]:

the snouting, velvet dingles   *the bucking ranches*
the lulled and dumbfound town   *the jollyrodgered sea*
the webfoot cocklewomen   *the anthracite statues*
the tidy wives   *the wetnosed yards*
the organplaying wood

Contrast Amis' *purposeful glances, smartly dressed youth, sheer bafflement, utter dedication*, where the premodifiers and nouns do collocate.

Hunched usually modifies animate beings, or parts of beings – *a hunched back*, rather than *a hunched wood*. *Snouting* in *snouting velvet dingles* refers, semantically, anaphorically back to the moles, rather than cataphorically forward to the inanimate dingles (anaphora and cataphora are discussed in Chapters 19 and 20 – they mean 'referring backward' and 'referring forward' in a text). *Organplaying* refers, semantically, anaphorically back to *rings, trousseaux, bridesmaided, aisles*, rather than cataphorically forward to the inanimate wood. *Ranches*, being inanimate, cannot *buck*, which usually collocates with horses. *Wetnosed* refers, semantically, anaphorically back to the *dogs*, rather than cataphorically forward to the inanimate *yards*.

People are usually *dumbfounded*, rather than an inanimate town, and the bare form *dumbfound* does not usually occur in premodifying position. Similarly the bare form *webfoot* does not usually occur in premodifying position, and *webfooted* usually collocates with types of birds, not women. There are two algorithms here:
1) place in front of the inanimate noun to come a modifier which collocates with the animate noun just mentioned
2) take a compound modifier which ends in *–ed*, dock the *–ed* and collocate it with something it does not usually collocate with

And what of the effect? That we can write algorithms for the Noun Phrase technique does not diminish Thomas' writing, it's mere fact. The effect, however, is subjective. *Under Milk Wood* has proved extremely popular – one of those texts which are more enduringly popular with the public at large than with present-day critics. This would suggest that listeners enjoy the animation conveyed by these surprises in the Noun Phrase.

4 Teaching Point

Premodification is not obligatory. It is possible to write a text without any premodification in the Noun Phrase at all. Therefore, when it is present, it is doing a job. What this job is will vary from text to text – and different readers will have different interpretations and different reactions.

3 On Adjectives

1 Definition of term *adjectives*

Adjectives typically modify a noun and sit in the Noun Phrase: they fit the testframe [*the very* _____ N]

> *the very green parrot*
> *the very old parrot*
> *the very excitable parrot*
> *the very squawking, shiny-feathered parrot*
> *the squawking-very-loudly-because-it-was-hungry parrot*/DT>

Adjectives can also sit in their own Adjective Phrase directly after the noun:

> *the parrot, green and shiny, made a noise*

Note how the whole unit [*green and shiny*], an Adjective Phrase, can be transposed before the noun:

> *The [green and shiny] parrot made a noise*

Adjectives can also sit in the testframe [*The* N *is* _____]

> *The parrot is green/old/excitable/squawking/shiny-feathered*

There are a few set phrases where the adjective always follows the noun:

> *the Princess Royal*
> *the Governor General*
> *from time immemorial*

Many adjectives can take comparative and superlative forms:

> *dry   drier   driest / most dry*
> *wet   wetter   wettest / most wet*

When analyzing Noun Phrases to identify the modifiers you will sometimes come across nouns which look like they are acting as adjectives – but which turn out not to be. Take *horse chestnut*, where *horse* modifies *chestnut* and tells us what sort of chestnut it is. However, the compound cannot take *very*: **the very horse chestnut*; there is no comparative or superlative form: **the horsier chestnut*; and the modifier cannot sit after the head noun: **the chestnut is horse*. *Horse chestnut* is therefore best analysed as a compound noun. However, from the point of view of literary analysis it is usually enough to spot the modifiers and their placement, regardless of whether that modifier be an adjective or a noun. In what follows, all Noun Phrase modifiers will be coloured, and their status as adjective or noun will be noted only if relevant to the discussion.

2 Demonstration of term *adjectives*

Read through the following passage and try to identify any adjective and noun modifiers. Can you see any patterns?

It was indeed a splendid road. It had been built by the natives, supervised by the Governor-General. He dreamt that on this beautiful road all Africa's wealth, its gold and diamonds and diverse mineral resources, its food, its energies, its labours, its intelligence would be transported to his land, to enrich the lives of his people across the green ocean.

Deep in his happy sleep the Governor-General dreamt of taking the Golden Stool of the Ashante king, the thinking masks of Bamako, the storytelling rocks of Zimbabwe, the symphonic Victoria Falls, the shapely tusks of Luo elephants, the slumbering trees of immemorial forests, the languorous river Niger, the enduring pyramids of the Nile, all the deltas rich with oil, the mountains rifted with metals apocalyptic, the mines shimmering with gold, the ancestral hills of Kilimanjaro, the lexicon of African rituals, the uncharted hinterland of Africa's unconquerable spirits. He dreamt of taking Africa's timber-like men, their pomegranate women, their fertile sculpture, their plaintive songs, their spirit-worlds, their forest animals, their sorceries, their myths and their strong dances. He dreamt that the natives would transport all these resources tangible and intangible, on their heads, or on litters, walking on the great road, in an orderly single file, across the Atlantic Ocean, for three thousand miles. He dreamt of having all these riches transported to his land. Some of them would be locked up in air-conditioned basements, for the benefit of Africa, because Africans did not know how to make the best use of them, and because his people could protect them better. He dreamt of having them in the basement of a great museum, to be studied, and to aid, in some obscure way, the progress of the human race.

Ben Okri, 1998, *Infinite Riches*

Here is the text again with the adjectives and nouns modifying nouns marked in orange.

It was indeed a splendid road. It had been built by the natives, supervised by the Governor-General. He dreamt that on this beautiful road all Africa's wealth, its gold and diamonds and diverse mineral resources, its food, its energies, its labours, its intelligence would be transported to his land, to enrich the lives of his people across the green ocean.

Deep in his happy sleep the Governor-General dreamt of taking the Golden Stool of the Ashante king, the thinking masks of Bamako, the storytelling rocks of Zimbabwe, the symphonic Victoria Falls, the shapely tusks of Luo elephants, the slumbering trees of immemorial forests, the languorous river Niger, the enduring pyramids of the Nile, all the deltas rich with oil, the mountains rifted with metals apocalyptic, the mines shimmering with gold, the ancestral hills of Kilimanjaro, the lexicon of African rituals, the uncharted hinterland of Africa's unconquerable spirits. He dreamt of taking Africa's timber-like men, their pomegranate women, their fertile sculpture, their plaintive songs, their spirit-worlds, their forest animals, their sorceries, their myths and their strong dances. He dreamt that the natives would transport all these resources tangible and intangible, on their heads, or on litters, walking on the great road, in an orderly single file, across the Atlantic Ocean, for three thousand miles. He dreamt of having all these riches transported to his land. Some of them would be locked up in air-conditioned basements, for the benefit of Africa, because Africans did not know how to make the best use of them, and because his people could protect them better. He dreamt of having them in the basement of a great museum, to be studied, and to aid, in some obscure way, the progress of the human race.

You may wonder why I have marked Ashante but not *Atlantic*. *Atlantic Ocean* is a Proper Noun (composed indeed of [Adj + N], deriving from Mount Atlas, on which the heavens were fabled to rest in Greek myth); the Noun Phrase [*Ashante king*] is not a Proper Noun in this context as the Golden Stool is the throne of all Ashante kings past and present.

Analysis

The placement is usually [Adj + N], with some exceptions: *resources tangible and intangible*, where the Adjective Phrase postmodifies the noun; and *the deltas* (which were) *rich, the mountains* (which were) *rifted, the mines* (which were) *shim-*

mering. Here, the relative pronouns which link clauses together (*which*) and the verbs (*were*) have been elided (you will meet verbs and relative pronouns in later chapters). There are two postposed adjectives: *Governor-General* and *metals apocalyptic*.

Many of the modifiers in the Governor-General's dream are ones which can only qualify animate beings, although in his dream they modify inanimate things: *happy* sleep, *thinking* masks, *storytelling* rocks, *slumbering* trees, *fertile* sculpture. By contrast, the humans in his dream are modified with inanimate nouns: *timber*(*like*) men and *pomegranate* women.

Commentary

The Governor-General is dreaming of something perverse – taking all the treasures from Africa and locking them up in a European basement – and his pairing of [animate modifier + inanimate noun] and [inanimate modifier + animate noun] mirrors this perversity.

3 Literary Exercise

In the following text, spot the adjective and noun modifiers. Can you find any patterns?

Black shadows fell on the water, echoes of nothing poured down the hills and steamed over the lake. It began to rain; a Swiss downpour soaked the earth. The flat bulbous vines about the hotel windows bled torrents over the ledges; the heads of the dahlias bent with the storm.

"How can they have the fête in the rain?" the children cried in dismay.

"Perhaps the ballet will wear their 'caoutchouc' as we have done," said Bonnie.

"I'd rather they had trained seals anyway," said the little boy optimistically.

The rain was a slow sparkling leak from a lachrymose sun. The wooden platforms about the estrade were damp and soaked with dye from the wet serpentine and sticky masses of confetti. Fresh wet light through the red and orange mushrooms of shiny umbrellas glowed like a lamp store display; a fashionable audience glistened in bright cellophane slickers.

"What if it rains down his horn?" said Bonnie, as the orchestra appeared beneath the rain-washed set of chinchilla-like mountains.

"But it might be pretty," protested the boy. "Sometimes in my bath when I sink beneath the water I make the most beautiful noises by blowing."

"It is ravishing," pronounced Genevra, "when my brother blows."

The damp air flattened the music like a sponge; girls brushed the rain from their hats; the rolling back of the tarred canvas exposed the slick and dangerous boards.

"It is Prometheus they're going to give," said David, reading the programme. "I will tell you the story afterwards."

From a whirr of revolving leaps Lorenz collected his brown magnificence, clenching his fists in the air and chinning the mystery of the mountain sky. His bare rain-polished body tortured itself to inextricable postures, straightened, and dropped to the floor with the suspended float of falling paper.

"Look, Bonnie," David called, "there's an old friend of yours!"

Arienne, subduing a technical maze of insolent turns and arrogant twists, represented a pink cupid. Damp and unconvincing, she tenaciously gripped the superhuman exigencies of her role. The workman underneath the artist ground out her difficult interpretation.

David felt an overwhelming unexpected surge of pity for the girl going through all that while the spectators thought of how wet they were getting and how uncomfortable they were. The dancers, too, were thinking of the rain, and shivered a little through the bursting crescendo of the finale.

Zelda Fitzgerald, 1932, *Save Me the Waltz*

Lexical note: *caoutchouc* and *slicker* were types of raincoat. An *estrade* is a slightly raised platform.

Analysis

Here is the text again with the the adjective and noun modifiers marked in orange.

Black shadows fell on the water, echoes of nothing poured down the hills and steamed over the lake. It began to rain; a Swiss downpour soaked the earth. The flat bulbous vines about the hotel windows bled torrents over the ledges; the heads of the dahlias bent with the storm.

"How can they have the fête in the rain?" the children cried in dismay.

"Perhaps the ballet will wear their 'caoutchouc' as we have done," said Bonnie.

"I'd rather they had trained seals anyway," said the little boy optimistically.

The rain was a slow sparkling leak from a lachrymose sun. The wooden platforms about the estrade were damp and soaked with dye from the wet serpentine and sticky masses of confetti. Fresh wet light through the red and orange mushrooms of shiny umbrellas glowed like a lamp store display; a fashionable audience glistened in bright cellophane slickers.

"What if it rains down his horn?" said Bonnie, as the orchestra appeared beneath the rain-washed set of chinchilla-like mountains.

"But it might be pretty," protested the boy. "Sometimes in my bath when I sink beneath the water I make the most beautiful noises by blowing."

"It is ravishing," pronounced Genevra, "when my brother blows."

The damp air flattened the music like a sponge; girls brushed the rain from their hats; the rolling back of the tarred canvas exposed the slick and dangerous boards.

"It is Prometheus they're going to give," said David, reading the programme. "I will tell you the story afterwards."

From a whirr of revolving leaps Lorenz collected his brown magnificence, clenching his fists in the air and chinning the mystery of the mountain sky. His bare rain-polished body tortured itself to inextricable postures, straightened, and dropped to the floor with the suspended float of falling paper.

"Look, Bonnie," David called, "there's an old friend of yours!"

Arienne, subduing a technical maze of insolent turns and arrogant twists, represented a pink cupid. Damp and unconvincing, she tenaciously gripped the superhuman exigencies of her role. The workman underneath the artist ground out her difficult interpretation.

David felt an overwhelming unexpected surge of pity for the girl going through all that while the spectators thought of how wet they were getting and how uncomfortable they were. The dancers, too, were thinking of the rain, and shivered a little through the bursting crescendo of the finale.

"I liked best the ones in black who fought themselves," said Bonnie.

"Yes," said the boy, "when they were bumping each other it was far best."

Commentary

There are two tokens (the technical term for 'instances') of [animate modifier + inanimate noun], *insolent* turns, *arrogant* twists, here serving to personify the danger of the dance in such slippery conditions. The adjectives fall into two main semantic groups, one to do with wet weather, and one to do with beauty:

> *lachrymose, damp, soaked, wet serpentine and sticky, fresh wet, rain-washed, damp, slick and dangerous, bare rain-polished, damp and unconvincing, wet, uncomfortable*

sparkling, shiny, fashionable, bright cellophane, chinchilla-like, pretty, most beautiful

The colours (*black, red, orange, brown, pink*) correlate with the second group. Although the ballet is a failure in that the audience and performers are soaked and neither group can concentrate, and Arienne's dance is laboured; nevertheless the rain lends a not-aesthetically-unpleasing quality to the fête, and the children's response is not negative. (That was a cumbersome sentence as piled-up negatives always are, but I'm trying to capture the seeing-something-good-in-a-dire-situation quality of the writing.) The sight of Arienne struggling under such adverse conditions provokes overwhelming emotion in David.

4 Teaching Point

Adjectives are very common in literary writing. Because they qualify and modify nouns, paying attention to them can focus your attention on nuances of meaning.

4 On Definite and Indefinite Articles

1 Definition of term the *Definite and Indefinite Article*

In Standard English writing, the indefinite article *a* is used before nouns beginning with a consonant, and *an* before nouns beginning with a vowel: *a* tomato, *an* axolotl. The indefinite article indicates a non-specific member of a group. The indefinite article *a, an* is in contradistinction to the definite article *the*, which indicates a specific member of a group: *the* tomato I'm eating now, *the* axolotl I'm picturing as I read. Collectively, the indefinite article and the definite article are grouped in a grammatical class known as *determiners*. Articles are very common in all text-types, yet authors can do interesting things with them.

2 Demonstration of the *Definite and Indefinite Article*

Here is an extract from a text containing many, but not an unusual amount of, articles. See if you can spot a significant shift from indefinite to definite (significant in the context of plot development, that is).

Somewhere in the register was written the name Elizabeth Hunt; but seventeen years after the entry the spoken name was Lizerunt. Lizerunt worked at a pickle factory, and appeared abroad in an elaborate and shabby costume, usually supplemented by a white apron. Withal she was something of a beauty. That is to say, her cheeks were very red, her teeth were very large and white, her nose was small and snub, and her fringe was long and shiny; while her face, new-washed, was susceptible of a high polish. Many such girls are married at sixteen, but Lizerunt was belated, and had never a bloke at all.

    Billy Chope was a year older than Lizerunt. He wore a billycock with a thin brim and a permanent dent in the crown; he had a bobtail coat, with the collar turned up at one side and down at the other, as an expression of independence; between his meals he carried his hands in his breeches pockets; and he lived with his mother, who mangled. His conversation with Lizerunt consisted long of perfunctory nods; but great things happened this especial Thursday evening, as Lizerunt, making for home, followed the fading red beyond the furthermost end of Commercial Road. For Billy Chope, slouching in the opposite direction, lurched across the pavement as they met, and taking the nearest hand from his pocket, caught and twisted her arm, bumping her against the wall.

"Garn," said Lizerunt, greatly pleased: "le' go!" For she knew that this was love.

"Where yer auf to, Lizer?"

"'Ome, o' course, cheeky. Le' go'" and she snatched – in vain – at Billy's hat.

Billy let go, and capered in front of her. She feigned to dodge by him, careful not to be too quick, because affairs were developing.

"I say, Lizer," said Billy, stopping his dance and becoming business-like, "going anywhere Monday?"

"Not along o' you, cheeky; you go 'long o' Beller Dawson, like wot you did Easter."

"Blow Beller Dawson; *she* ain't no good. I'm goin' on the Flats. Come?"

Lizerunt, delighted but derisive, ended with a promise to "see." The bloke had come at last, and she walked home with the feeling of having taken her degree. She had half assured herself of it two days before, when Sam Cardew threw an orange peel at her, but went away after a little prancing on the pavement. Sam was a smarter fellow than Billy, and earned his own living; probably his attentions were serious; but one must prefer the bird in hand. As for Billy Chope, he went his way, resolved himself to take home what mangling he should find his mother had finished, and stick to the money; also, to get all he could from her by blandishing and bullying, that the jaunt to Wanstead Flats might be adequately done.

There is no other fair like Whit Monday's on Wanstead Flats. Here is a square mile and more of open land where you may howl at large; here is no danger of losing yourself as in Epping Forest; the public-houses are always with you; shows, shines, swings, merry-go-rounds, fried-fish stalls, donkeys are packed closer than on Hampstead Heath; the ladies' tormentors are larger, and their contents smell worse than at any other fair. Also, you may be drunk and disorderly without being locked up – for the stations won't hold everybody – and when all else has palled, you may set fire to the turf. Hereinto Billy and Lizerunt projected themselves from the doors of the Holly Tree on Whit Monday morning. But through hours on hours of fried fish and half-pints both were conscious of a deficiency. For the hat of Lizerunt was brown and old; plush it was not, and its feather was a mere foot long and of a very rusty black. Now, it is not decent for a factory girl from Limehouse to go bank-holidaying under any but a hat of plush, very high in the crown, of a wild blue or a wilder green, and carrying withal an ostrich feather, pink or scarlet or what not; a feather that springs from the fore-part, climbs the crown, and drops as far down the shoulders as may be. Lizerunt knew this, and, had she had no bloke, would have stayed at home. But a chance is a chance. As it was, only another such hapless girl could measure her bitter envy of the feathers about her, or would so joyfully have given an ear for the proper splendor. Billy, too, had a vague impression, muddled by but not drowned in half-pints, that some degree of plush was condign to the occasion and to his own expenditure. Still, there was no quarrel; and the pair walked and ran with arms about each other's necks; and Lizerunt thumped her bloke on the back at proper intervals; so that the affair went regularly on the whole: although, in view of Lizerunt's shortcomings, Billy did not insist on the customary exchange of hats.

Everything, I say, went well and well enough until Billy bought a ladies' tormentor and began to squirt it at Lizerunt. For then Lizerunt went scampering madly, with piercing shrieks, until her bloke was left some little way behind, and Sam Cardew, turning up at that moment, and seeing her running alone in the crowd, threw his arms about her waist and swung her round him again and again, as he floundered gallantly this way and that, among the shies and the hokeypokey barrows.

Arthur Morrison. 1894. *Tales of Mean Streets*

Note on dialect: the dialogue is written in London English, which is *h*-deleting in word-initial position, and *r*-inserting when words begin and end with a vowel. The short form of Elizabeth, *Liza*, together with *h*-deletion of *Hunt*, and *r*-insertion between words ending and beginning with a vowel, gives *Lizerunt*. *Garn* is 'go on'. *Stations* is short for police-stations. Some of the vocabulary has since fallen out of use since 1894:

> *Oxford English Dictionary* tormentor, *n.* 3. f. *ladies' tormentor* 'a device used to annoy at pleasure-fairs (frequently a device for squirting liquid)', attested 1891–1912.
>
> *Oxford English Dictionary* hokeypokey, *n.* 2. 'a cheap kind of ice-cream sold by street vendors', attested 1884–1970.
>
> *Oxford English Dictionary* shine, $n.^2$ 'a party, convivial gathering', attested 1838–1882.

Commentary

"Lizerunt was belated, and had never a bloke at all" at the end of paragraph one, becomes "The bloke had come at last" after the passage of dialogue. The indefinite *a bloke* could signify Billy Chope or Sam Cardew, and at the start of the text Lizerunt inclines to think it is likely to be Sam, but it turns out definitely to be Billy, and so he becomes *the bloke*. A small transaction linguistically but a crucial transition, and the plot can now develop as Sam Cardew arrives back on the scene to rival Billy.

3 Literary Exercise

See if you can spot something clever in the following extract with regard to the indefinite article:

Ida went into a pub and had a glass of Douro port. It went down sweet and warm and heavy. She had another. 'Who's Mr Colleoni?' she asked the barman.
　'You don't know who Colleoni is?'
　'I never heard of him till just now.'
　The barman said, 'He's taking over from Kite.'
　'Who's Kite?'
　'Who *was* Kite? You saw how he got croaked at St Pancras?'
　'No.'
　'I don't suppose they meant to do it,' the barman said. 'They just meant to carve him up, but a razor slipped.'
　'Have a drink?'
　'Thanks. I'll have a gin.'
　'Cheeryo.'
　'Cheeryo.'
　'I hadn't heard all this,' Ida said. She looked over his shoulder at the clock: nothing to do till one: she might as well have another and gossip awhile. 'Give me another port. When did all this happen?'
　'Oh, before Whitsun.' The word Whitsun always caught her ear now: it meant a lot of things, a grubby ten shilling note, the white steps down to the ladies', Tragedy in capital letters. 'And what about Kite's friends?' she asked.
　'They don't stand a chance now Kite's dead. The mob's got no leader. Why, they tag round after a kid of seventeen. What's a kid like that going to do against Colleoni?' He bent across the bar and whispered, 'He cut up Brewer last night.'
　'Who? Colleoni?'
　'No, the kid.'
　'I dunno who Brewer is,' Ida said, 'but things seem lively.'
　'You wait till the races start,' the man said. 'They'll be lively all right then. Colleoni's out for a monopoly. Quick, look through the window there and you'll see him.'
　Ida went to the window and looked out, and again she saw only the Brighton she knew; she hadn't seen anything different even the day Fred died: two girls in beach pyjamas arm-in-arm, the buses going by to Rottingdean, a man selling papers,

a woman with a shopping basket, a boy in a shabby suit, an excursion steamer edging off from the pier, which lay long, luminous and transparent, like a shrimp in the sunlight. She said, 'I don't see anyone.'

'He's gone now.'

'Who? Colleoni?'

'No, the kid.'

'Oh,' Ida said, 'that boy,' coming back to the bar, drinking up her port.

Graham Greene, 1938, *Brighton Rock*

Analysis

'That boy' is Pinkie, who has taken over as the leader of Kite's mob after Kite was killed. Mr Colleoni is the leader of the rival mob who killed Kite. But Ida doesn't know any of this.

> Ida went to the window and looked out, and again she saw only the Brighton she knew; she hadn't seen anything different even the day Fred died: two girls in beach pyjamas arm-in-arm, the buses going by to Rottingdean, a man selling papers, a woman with a shopping basket, a boy in a shabby suit, an excursion steamer edging off from the pier, which lay long, luminous and transparent, like a shrimp in the sunlight.

In this sentence there are six uncoordinated Noun Phrases (*uncoordinated* means without an explicit link like *and*); their determiners, premodifiers and heads being *two girls, the buses, a man, a woman, a boy, an excursion steamer.* Here are the postmodifiers: [*in beach pyjamas*] [*arm-in-arm*], [*going by to Rottingdean*], [*selling papers*], [*with a shopping basket*], [*in a shabby suit*], [*edging off from the pier,*] [*which lay long, luminous and transparent,*] [*like a shrimp in the sunlight*]. The first and the last Noun Phrases in the list are the heaviest (having more than one postmodifier), and the four in the middle are light, so they can be represented in size as XxxxxX:

NP 1. [two girls] [in beach pyjamas] [arm-in-arm]
NP 2. [the buses] [going by to Rottingdean]
NP 3. [a man] [selling papers]
NP 4. [a woman] [with a shopping basket]
NP 5. [a boy] [in a shabby suit]
NP 6. [an excursion steamer] [edging off from the pier,] [which lay long, luminous and transparent,] [like a shrimp in the sunlight]

Thus there are two heavy book-ends, and a list of four lighter Noun Phrases in the middle, where the determiner sequence moves from the specific definite article of *the* buses to the generic indefinite articles of *a* man, *a* woman, *a* boy, in anthropologically prototypical descending order. This renders the last light x the least important and least noticeable slot of all in the list of Noun Phrases – and along with Ida, many a reader will fail to notice the significance of *a boy in a shabby suit* on first reading.

Commentary

Greene has buried the shabby-suited Pinkie in the least noticeable position in the list of Noun Phrases. Mr Colleoni has a notoriety, presence and glamour which Pinkie lacks, and covets.

4 Teaching Point

Authors will use a great quantity of determiners, most of which are unlikely to be of significance from the point of view of literary criticism. But any binary code contains the possibility of comparison, of juxtaposition or contradistinction, and so *a* can be contrasted with *the* (as in Arthur Morrison's text), or used to lull the reader (as with Grahame Greene's).

5 Personal Pronouns

1 Definition of term *Personal Pronouns*

Personal pronouns are small words which can stand in for nouns:

> The sun is shining. It is early Spring.

It refers anaphorically back to the sun and lets me avoid repetition. The personal pronouns used in Subject position (when they govern a verb) are:

Person	Singular	Plural
1st	*I*	*we*
2nd	*you*	*you*
3rd	*he/she/it*	*they*

e.g. *It is Spring; I like Spring*

When personal pronouns are used in Object position (when they are the recipient of the action of the verb) they change to:

Person	Singular	Plural
1st	*me*	*us*
2nd	*you*	*you*
3rd	*him/her/it*	*them*

e.g. *Spring cheers me; Spring warms us.*

When personal pronouns are used as Possessives, they change to:

Person	Singular	Plural
1st	*mine*	*ours*
2nd	*yours*	*yours*
3rd	*his/hers/its*	*theirs*

e.g. *These daffodils are ours but those ones are theirs.*

2 Demonstration of *Personal Pronouns*

Read this text and see if you can spot the pronouns.

                       N.W.2: Spring
The poets never lied when they praised
Spring in England.
                       Even in this neat suburb
You can feel there's something to
                                their pastorals.
Something gentle, broadly nostalgic, is stirring
On the well-aired pavements.
                       Indrawn brick
Sighs, and you notice the sudden sharpness
Of things growing.
                     The sun lightens
The significance of what the houses
Are steeped in,
               Brightens out
Their winter brooding.
                   Early May
Touches also the cold diasporas
That England hardly mentions.

A. C. Jacobs, 1976, *N.W.2: Spring*

Note: What is the significance of the layout? Is it reflecting the patterns of brickwork?

Here is the text again, this time with the pronouns in green:

The poets never lied when they praised
Spring in England.
                     Even in this neat suburb
You can feel there's something to
                              their pastorals.
Something gentle, broadly nostalgic, is stirring
On the well-aired pavements.
                       Indrawn brick
Sighs, and you notice the sudden sharpness
Of things growing.
                     The sun lightens
The significance of what the houses
Are steeped in,
               Brightens out

>   Their winter brooding.
>   Early May
>   Touches also the cold diasporas
>   That England hardly mentions.

A. C. Jacobs (1937–94) was born in Scotland of Jewish parents and lived for a time in Jerusalem, and for a time in Hendon, London, N.W.2, where he was a schoolboy.

The poets never lied when they praised / Spring in England.

They refers anaphorically back to 'the poets'. Notice the colloquial tone of *never lied* – *never* as a negator is present in all the regional dialects, as in "Did you steal my rubber?" "No I never!", meaning not on this occasion, as opposed to the Standard English sense of on every occasion. "The poets never lied" may be literal, i.e. they did not lie on each and every occasion they praised Spring, but this use of [*never* + V] cannot avoid sounding colloquial.

Even in this neat suburb / You can feel there's something to / their pastorals.

Their refers back to the works of the poets praising Spring. But who is the *you*? Standard English has an impersonal third-person pronoun, *one*, but many speakers do not use it and find it slightly offensive. (You will know whether you avoid *one* and notice it each time you hear it, or whether you don't really notice it, in which case you probably do have it in your own personal version of English, your idiolect.) *One* often sounds formal, and we've already seen that the tone of this poem is not formal. Speakers can avail themselves of *you* as an alternative for *one*; however, the narrator might be addressing the reader at this point, suggesting that the reader also feels the aptness of the paeans to Spring in England, in which case *you* would be a second-person singular pronoun rather than a third-person singular one. I'm inclined to read it as a third-person usage, but whichever, use of *you* includes the reader to a greater (second-person) or lesser (third-person) degree, and maintains the non-formal tone. This move away from formal poetic language is continued with the elision *there's*, with the colloquial idiom *there's something to (it)*, and also with the phrase *neat suburb*, the word *suburb* not usually occurring in canonical poetry.

Indrawn brick / Sighs, and you notice the sudden sharpness / Of things growing.

Or should we be interpreting *you* as a first-person pronoun? The verbs *feel* and *notice* are 'interior state' verbs, that is, other people cannot know what someone else is feeling or noticing. The narrator finds himself able to feel Spring in N.W.2, and to notice the sudden sharpness of things growing there. Like third-person usage, saying *you* to mean yourself is common in informal speech. The rather unpoetic tone continues (*things growing*, rather than a more florid description of the burgeoning greenery), and some more ambiguities: is the sharpness due to the clarity provided by the Spring sun low in the sky? What is indrawn brick and how does it sigh? My guess is that the brick which has been holding its breath all winter relaxes in the Spring sunshine.

> The sun lightens / The significance of what the houses / Are steeped in, / Brightens out / Their winter brooding.

Their refers back to 'the houses'. They have been brooding all winter (presumably 'mulling over in a rather negative way', rather than 'sitting on eggs', although there is a result implicit in brooding eggs), but what is the significance? Is cold and damp what they are steeped in? In which case, what is the significance of the cold and damp? The final three lines tell us where this significance may lie, and what it may be:

> Early May / Touches also the cold diasporas / That England hardly mentions.

The diasporas, in the context of N.W.2, refer to the dispersal of the Jewish people around the globe, as Jews settled in that part of North London during and after the Second World War. England hardly mentions these cold diasporas, but the thoughts of the narrator are with the scattered Jews: not in Israel, no longer in bourgeois Vienna or Salzburg or Cologne, nor in the ghettoes and shtetls of Central and Eastern Europe, but displaced from New York to New Zealand. A. C. Jacobs' use of *you* encompasses first, second and third-person usage. As we read through the body of the poem most readers will, to some extent, enter into agreement with the narrator, partly because of identifying ourselves with *you*, partly because of the colloquial tone, and perhaps because of also liking poems about Spring or Spring in a suburb. However, a subset of readers, those who are keen to disassociate themselves with Jews, will differ sharply at the end – despite having experienced the kinds of agreement mentioned, up to that point.

3 Literary Exercise

Identify the personal pronouns in the following extract from Derek Walcott's poem *Omeros*. What do they contribute to the poem?

In scorched summer light, from the circle of Charing Cross,
he arose with the Underground's grit and its embers of sparrows
in a bargeman's black greatcoat, clutching in one scrofulous

claw his brown paper manuscript. The nose, like a pharos,
bulbed from his cragged face, and the beard under it was
foam that exploded into the spray burst of eyebrows.

On the verge of collapse, the fallen sails of his trousers
were upheld by a rope. In the barges of different shoes
he flapped towards the National. The winch of his voice,

a fog still in its throat, barged through the queues
at the newspaper kiosks, then changed gears with the noise
of red double-deckers embarking on chartered views

from pigeon-stirred Trafalgar; it broke off the icing
from wedding-cake London. Gryphons on their ridge
of sandstone snarled because it had carried the cries in

the Isle of Dogs running over Westminster Bridge.
Today it would anchor in the stone waves of the entrance
of St. Martin-in-the-Fields. There, in tiered sunshine,

the black sail collapsed, face sunward with both hands
crossed over the shop-paper volume bound with grey twine.
He looked like a heap of slag-coal crusting the tiers

with their summering tourists. Eyes shut, the frayed lips
chewed the breeze, the beard curled like the dog's ears
of his turned-down *Odyssey*, but Omeros was naming the ships

whose oars spidered soundlessly over the sun-webbed calm
behind his own lashes. Then, suddenly, a raging sparrow
of a church-warden bobbed down the steps. It picked one arm.

The bargeman huddled. It screeched. It yanked an elbow,
then kicked him with polished pumps, and a curse as
Greek to the choleric cleric as one might imagine

sprayed the spluttering soutane. It showed him the verses
framed at the entrance announcing this Sunday's lesson
in charity, etc. Then, like a dromedary, over the sands

of the scorching pavement, the hump began to press on
back to the river. The sparrow, rubbing both hands,
nodded, and chirruped up the steps back to its sanctuary,

> where, dipping one claw in the font, it vanished inside
> the webbed stone. The bargeman tacked towards his estuary
> of light. It was summer. London rustled with pride.
>
> Derek Walcott, 1990, *Omeros*, Chapter XXXVIII/I

Lexical note: *pharos* is Latin for 'lighthouse', from the name of a Greek island.

Here is the text again, with the pronouns in green:

> In scorched summer light, from the circle of Charing Cross,
> he arose with the Underground's grit and its embers of sparrows
> in a bargeman's black greatcoat, clutching in one scrofulous
>
> claw his brown paper manuscript. The nose, like a pharos,
> bulbed from his cragged face, and the beard under it was
> foam that exploded into the spray burst of eyebrows.
>
> On the verge of collapse, the fallen sails of his trousers
> were upheld by a rope. In the barges of different shoes
> he flapped towards the National. The winch of his voice,
>
> a fog still in its throat, barged through the queues
> at the newspaper kiosks, then changed gears with the noise
> of red double-deckers embarking on chartered views
>
> from pigeon-stirred Trafalgar; it broke off the icing
> from wedding-cake London. Gryphons on their ridge
> of sandstone snarled because it had carried the cries in
>
> the Isle of Dogs running over Westminster Bridge.
> Today it would anchor in the stone waves of the entrance
> of St. Martin-in-the-Fields. There, in tiered sunshine,
>
> the black sail collapsed, face sunward with both hands
> crossed over the shop-paper volume bound with grey twine.
> He looked like a heap of slag-coal crusting the tiers
>
> with their summering tourists. Eyes shut, the frayed lips
> chewed the breeze, the beard curled like the dog's ears
> of his turned-down *Odyssey*, but Omeros was naming the ships
>
> whose oars spidered soundlessly over the sun-webbed calm
> behind his own lashes. Then, suddenly, a raging sparrow
> of a church-warden bobbed down the steps. It picked one arm.
>
> The bargeman huddled. It screeched. It yanked an elbow,
> then kicked him with polished pumps, and a curse as
> Greek to the choleric cleric as one might imagine

sprayed the spluttering soutane. It showed him the verses
framed at the entrance announcing this Sunday's lesson
in charity, etc. Then, like a dromedary, over the sands

of the scorching pavement, the hump began to press on
back to the river. The sparrow, rubbing both hands,
nodded, and chirruped up the steps back to its sanctuary,

where, dipping one claw in the font, it vanished inside
the webbed stone. The bargeman tacked towards his estuary
of light. It was summer. London rustled with pride.

Analysis

He, the bargeman, Omeros, emerges from the underground at Charing Cross, walks towards the National Gallery, and lies down on the steps of the church of St Martin-in-the-Fields, which is tiered like a wedding cake. He is singing or talking or shouting as he walks, the winch (of his voice) barging through queues, changing gear, breaking off stonework (the icing), being snarled at by sandstone Gryphons, and finally anchoring on the steps of St Martin-in-the-Fields. There, as he dozes, a raging sparrow (of a churchwarden) picks his arm, screeches, yanks his elbow, kicks him, shows him the notices at the entrance, and then when Omeros leaves, goes back inside. What one might expect to be the head noun of the Noun Phrase (*voice, churchwarden*) postmodifies other nouns (*winch, sparrow*), and it is the head nouns *winch* and *sparrow* that are trailed by anaphoric pronouns. This causes a clash between human/non-human referents: a churchwarden would normally be referred to as *he*, but a sparrow as *it*. There is a further clash with possessive *his* (*his estuary of light*), humans not normally owning estuaries, nor estuaries being of light. The final *it* in the last line is known as 'dummy *it*'. English has two dummy forms, *it* and *there*, also known as 'existential *there/it*'. They are subject place-holders and have no semantic content.

Commentary

The metaphor for Omeros is of the watery world of ships and shipping. The action is of a tramp walking along one side of Trafalgar Square and being removed from the church steps by a churchwarden. The churchwarden is ornithomorphised as a sparrow, a land bird rather than a seabird (sparrows used to be associated with London although few now remain). The social hierarchy (churchwarden = high, tramp = low) is reversed by the pronouns (tramp = *he*, sparrow = *it*). Although we hear the poem through the voice of the narrator, the narrator is on Omeros's side.

4 Teaching Point

Although pronouns form what linguists call a 'closed class', that is, authors can't invent more, speakers and writers can use pronouns in multiple and versatile ways. *You* and *we* are particularly malleable. In a given context, is *we* inclusive: 'Yay! We're off to the seaside!', or exclusive: 'We're off tomorrow so will you water the plants?'

6 Prepositional Phrases

1 Definition of term *Prepositional Phrases*

Prepositions can be described as small words which serve to anchor in time and space – *in, to, at, by, for, of, out, with, over, under, between, across, beside, along, until, during, through, before, without, throughout, atop, beneath* ... although the most frequent preposition in English, *of*, just to be perverse, is neither spatial nor temporal.

The following test frames usually work for prepositions:

_____ the road	*on the road, beside the road, under the road, over the road, to the road, through the road, across the road, beneath the road, atop the road*
_____ the hour	*on the hour, within the hour, by the hour, for the hour, of the hour, at the hour, until the hour, during the hour, through the hour, throughout the hour*

Prepositions can also occur in groups, known as complex prepositions:

in front of, by way of, with a view to, in lieu of

Prepositions typically precede nouns, and we call the whole construction a Prepositional Phrase:

by the platform

[[by]Preposition [the platform]Noun Phrase]] Prepositional Phrase

Prepositions sometimes govern units containing a verb, and we call those constructions Prepositional Clauses:

by running quickly

[[by]Preposition [[running]Verb Phrase] quickly]]Prepositional Clause

She caught the train [by the platform]Prepositional Phrase [by running quickly] Prepositional Clause

She caught the train (by the platform) (by running quickly)
                                    Prepositional Phrase   *Prepositional Clause*

Prepositions also sit after some verbs, which are known as Phrasal Verbs:

to go out, to go in, to go up, to go down, to go through, to do in, to put up, to put up with, to let in, to let up

2 Demonstration of Prepositional Phrases

Here is an extract from a script for a television programme made by John Betjeman in 1972 about people going to Southend on Sundays. The Prepositional Phrases are highlighted in green (with a few other prepositional constructions in blue)

Vision	Commentary
Aerial tracking shot of Fenchurch Street Station and along the line.	What do most Londoners do [on Sunday]? They leave it. Most comfortably of course [by rail] [from Fenchurch Street]
London houses and flats seen from the train.	[over brick arches]. Who would want to stay behind [in an inhuman slab] [of council flats], built [in the priggish
People travelling in a bus. A bicycle on top of a car.	1960s], when sea and country call? We leave [by every means] we can.
A station and rail track seen from the train. Close-ups of a bus and car wheels.	Swift, swiftly eastwards [through Stepney, Barking, Dagenham, Upminster], electric railway, diesel coach and bus, car and motorbike, bypass and high road.
Outer London suburbs seen from the train, revealing Essex.	Eastward and further east [until the last brick box] is [out of sight], and then we see the wide enormous marsh [of Essex],
A boy on a motorbike and a family in a car.	London's nearest real countryside, and join the others speeding [to Southend].
Interior of a family in a Southend Pier tram. The sea from the window.	Hold on, what's that? A different sort [of noise]. And now we're [in a different sort] [of train]. We're travelling [down Southend Pier] [by tram], [for a mile and a third] [towards the coast] [of France]. The longest pier [in the world]. Was it perhaps a mid-Victorian dream [of bringing England close to France]
A couple walking along the pier in the wind.	[at last], and getting there [on foot]? Or was it to build an elongated jetty
A man walking under the pier.	[for vessels] making [for the Thames's mouth]?
Men walking under the pier. Mid-shot of the pier end and close-up of fishermen's faces and tackle.	[At any rate], today [upon the pier] they sell a map which shows you where to find the different kinds [of fish] the estuary yields and what's the bait to use. [To southward] [from Southend] [across the Thames]
Long shot of a boat against oil refineries.	you faintly see [along the Kentish coast] the oil refineries which work [on Sunday]. Give me Sunday here,
A man sitting on the pier. A child with a thermos flask and men fishing.	sniffing the salt sea air and salt sea water. Sundays [of patience] waiting [for a bite].
A couple pushing a pram. A courting couple.	Sunday the day when fathers push the pram. Sunday [for lovers] walking [in the wind].
A father running with two small children.	Sunday [for running] to catch the lunchtime tram.
A tram.	And missing it.

(continued)

Vision	Commentary
Leaving the terminus.	It doesn't matter here, time's [of no consequence] [in kind Southend]. An unpretentious, breezy, friendly place. I like Southend. East London [on the sea].
The reverse of the tram trundling back along the pier in the sea.	Southend where Charlie Chaplin as a child first saw the real sea and thought it was a wall [of sky-blue water].

Extract from John Betjeman, 1972, *Thank God it's Sunday*

of course is an Adverbial Phrase (see Chapter 14)

stay behind, hold on, make for, are Phrasal Verbs (see Chapter 8)

to stay, to use, to build, to find, to catch are what linguists call '*to* + base form' (you might know it as the *infinitive*), a nonfinite form. *Finite* means being marked for person, tense and number (see Chapter 7), so nonfinite forms are timeless – Betjeman is talking about all Sundays.

of bringing England close to France is a nonfinite Prepositional Clause, due to the presence of *bringing* (see Chapter 18)

Prepositions anchor a text in time and place. Here, the time is Sundays, the place consists of various locations on the way to, and at, Southend. If you run your eye over the text in green, you'll see that this is the part of the text that details those times and places.

3 Literary Exercise

Here H. G. Wells describes a monkey-parade in a thinly-disguised Beckenham, South London. A monkey-parade was an evening teenagers' promenade. They died out after World War II. Can you identify the prepositional phrases and clauses? What kind of information do they contain?

It was in that phase of an urban youth's development, the phase of the cheap cigarette, that this thing happened. One evening I came by chance on a number of young people promenading by the light of a row of shops towards Beckington, and, with all the glory of a glowing cigarette between my lips, I joined their strolling number. These twilight parades of young people, youngsters chiefly of the lower middle-class, are one of the odd social developments of the great suburban growths – unkindly critics, blind to the inner meanings of things, call them, I believe, Monkeys' Parades – the shop apprentices, the young work girls, the boy clerks and so forth, stirred by mysterious intimations, spend their first-earned money upon collars and ties, chiffon hats, smart lace collars, walking-sticks, sunshades or cigarettes, and come valiantly into the vague transfiguring mingling of gaslight and evening, to walk up and down, to eye meaningly, even to accost and make friends. It is a queer instinctive revolt from the narrow limited friendless homes in which so many find themselves, a going out towards something, romance if you will, beauty, that has suddenly become a need – a need that hitherto has lain dormant and unsuspected. They promenade.

Vulgar! – it is as vulgar as the spirit that calls the moth abroad in the evening and lights the body of the glow-worm in the night. I made my way through the throng, a little contemptuously as became a public schoolboy, my hands in my pockets – none of your cheap canes for me! – and very careful of the lie of my cigarette upon my lips. And two girls passed me, one a little taller than the other, with dim warm-tinted faces under clouds of dark hair and with dark eyes like pools reflecting stars.

I half turned, and the shorter one glanced back at me over her shoulder – I could draw you now the pose of her cheek and neck and shoulder – and instantly I was as passionately in love with the girl as I have ever been before or since, as any man ever was with any woman. I turned about and followed them, I flung away my cigarette ostentatiously and lifted my school cap and spoke to them.

H. G. Wells, 1910, *The New Machiavelli*.

Here is the text again, with the prepositional phrases in green and other prepositional constructions in blue.

It was [in that phase] [of an urban youth's development], the phase [of the cheap cigarette], that this thing happened. One evening I came [by chance] [on a number of young people] promenading [by the light] [of a row] [of shops] [towards Beckington], and, [with all the glory] [of a glowing cigarette] [between my lips], I joined their strolling number. These twilight parades [of young people], youngsters chiefly [of the lower middle-class], are one [of the odd social developments] [of the great suburban growths] – unkindly critics, blind [to the inner meanings] [of things], call them, I believe, Monkeys' Parades – the shop apprentices, the young work girls, the boy clerks and so forth, stirred [by mysterious intimations], spend their first-earned money [upon collars and ties, chiffon hats, smart lace collars, walking-sticks, sunshades or cigarettes], and come valiantly [into the vague transfiguring mingling] [of gaslight and evening], to walk up and down, to eye meaningly, even to accost and make friends. It is a queer instinctive revolt [from the narrow limited friendless homes] [in which so many find themselves], a going out [towards something, romance if you will, beauty], that has suddenly become a need – a need that hitherto has lain dormant and unsuspected. They promenade.

Vulgar! – it is as vulgar as the spirit that calls the moth abroad [in the evening] and lights the body [of the glow-worm] [in the night]. I made my way [through the throng], a little contemptuously as became a public schoolboy, my hands [in my pockets] – none [of your cheap canes] [for me!] – and very careful [of the lie] [of my cigarette] [upon my lips]. And two girls passed me, one a little taller than the other, with dim warm-tinted faces [under clouds of dark hair] and [with dark eyes like pools reflecting stars].

I half turned, and the shorter one glanced back [at me] [over her shoulder] – I could draw you now the pose [of her cheek and neck and shoulder] – and instantly I was as passionately [in love] [with the girl] as I have ever been before or since, as any man ever was [with any woman]. I turned about and followed them, I flung away my cigarette ostentatiously and lifted my school cap and spoke [to them].

to walk up, to walk down, to go out, to call abroad, to glance back, to turn about, to fling away – these are Phrasal Verbs made up of [verb + preposition], all linking the action to the place (see Chapter 8 for more on Phrasal Verbs).

Analysis

The Prepositional Phrases in this extract are governed by the prepositions in, of, by, on, towards, with, between, to, upon, into, from, through, under, over. The promenading boys and girls themselves are mentioned in Noun Phrases, but the Prepositional Phrases tell us why, how, and with what they attract attention. Why: as with other creatures (moths, monkeys, glow-worms), they are stirred [by mysterious intimations], [towards something, romance, beauty]; **where**: [into the vague transfiguring mingling] [of gaslight and evening], [by the light] [of a row] [of shops] [towards Beckington]; **how**: with various accessories [of the cheap cigarette], [of a glowing cigarette], [upon collars and ties, chiffon hats, smart lace collars, walking-sticks, sunshades or cigarettes], [of your cheap canes], [of my cigarette]. The details of the mating ritual (in which cigarettes played quite a role, hence the five mentions) are largely communicated via the Prepositional Phrase.

Commentary

Why is the observation that this particular information is conveyed in this syntactic construction relevant? Wells has to work hard here, because to the contemporary readership in 1910 the term *monkey parade* was well-known and derogatory (compare *cattle market* today). Debutantes' balls, although having exactly the same function, were not derided as monkey parades, because they were about securing the future of the wealth of the upper classes. Wells is making a causal relationship between the lower-middle-class boys and girls and their accoutrements: it is because they are boys and girls that they have, as a biological imperative, to try to attract one another. The schoolboy's use of his cigarette to heighten his attraction – to look cool – is both aligned with the natural world, the moths and the glow-worms, and with high culture (*valiantly, beauty, romance; as any man ever was with any woman*). Prepositions are linking devices, relating one thing to another. Wells uses them to persuade the reader that the lower-class monkey parade is, on the one hand, no different from a bird's bright plumage or mating dance, and on the other, in the tradition of high literary culture.

4 Teaching Point

Prepositional Phrases convey detail that anchors the text in time and space. They are in almost every text and easy to overlook. They point you to when, where and how – so if you find a preponderance of prepositions, it's worth considering their focus.

7 On Verbs: Tense

1 Definition of term *Tense*

Verbs in present-day English change their form depending on whether they are expressing past or present states: I *skulk* (now), I *skulked* (then); I *thrive* (now), I *throve* (then). There is one further suffix in present-day Standard English, the third person singular present ending -*s*: he/she/it/one *skulks*. And that's it. There are no more suffixes to be added to the verb to express when the action took place.

Note on terminology: linguists refer to the '-*ed* form' for the past, even when it is the vowel that changes rather than a suffix added, as in *throve*.

Verbs which are marked to express a time-period are called *finite* verbs. Finite verbs in English can be marked with –*ed*, -*s* or zero, and can express past or present time.

	Present				Past		
Singular		*plural*		*singular*		*Plural*	
I	0	we	0	I	-ed	we	-ed
You	0	you	0	you	-ed	you	-ed
he/she/it	-s	they	0	he/she/it	-ed	they	-ed

If we want to express futurity, we have to use a time-referring verb, known as an *auxiliary*: I *will* skulk, I *shall* skulk, or express it another way: I *am going* to skulk, *tomorrow* it is my intention to skulk. There is no ending, or vowel change, that we can add to the verb itself to express futurity. Present-day English has two tenses that are expressed *morphologically*, past and present. [A morpheme is the smallest grammatical unit; in this case, zero, -*s* and –*ed*.]

Rather than the term 'present', linguists use the term 'non-past' instead. This is because the present tense form is used for past, present and future states:

Water boils at 100 degrees	it always has boiled, boils now, and will boil in the future at 100 degrees
On Monday I fly to Helsinki	Monday is in the future
I read my email every day	I have read my email every day in the past up til now, and probably will in future, a habitual action

2 Demonstration of *Tense: Non-Past*

Consider the time-periods expressed by the finite verbs in the following extract:

As an apprentice to lighthouse-keeping my duties were as follows:
1) Brew a pot of Full Strength Samson and take it to Pew.
2) 8 am. Take DogJim for a walk.
3) 9 am. Cook bacon.
4) 10 am. Sluice the stairs.
5) 11 am. More tea.
6) Noon. Polish the instruments.
7) 1 pm. Chops and tomato sauce.
8) 2 pm. Lesson – History of Lighthouses.
9) 3 pm. Wash our socks etc.
10) 4 pm. More tea.
11) 5 pm. Walk the dog and collect supplies.
12) 6 pm. Pew cooks supper.
13) 7 pm. Pew sets the light. I watch.
14) 8 pm. Pew tells me a story.
15) 9 pm. Pew tends the light. Bed.

Jeanette Winterson, 2004, *Lighthousekeeping*.

These are all habitual actions, going back to whenever the apprentice began work and projecting into the future: what I have always done since I became an apprentice lighthouse-keeper and what I shall do until my apprenticeship ends. The verbs *brew, take, cook, sluice, polish, wash, walk* and *collect*, base forms, are a list of instructions. [Instructions, orders and commands are known as *imperatives*.] However *cooks, sets, tells, tends* are marked with third person singular *–s*, and *watch*, although zero-marked, is governed by the pronoun *I*, so the verbs in 12–15 are all finite, marked for the non-past. One could then, retrospectively, read the previous verbs as though they were governed by *I* too – in which case, they too would be non-past rather than imperatives; i.e. 'I brew a pot of Full Strength Samson and take it to Pew, I take DogJim for a walk'.

What is the effect? Beginning reading the text as a set of imperative commands which then veer to finite forms lends a certain bathos (*bathos*: 'anticlimax, descent from the elevated to the commonplace'). The imperative style is naval (*sluice the stairs, polish the instruments, collect supplies*), as is the vocabulary (*sluice* rather than *clean; collect supplies* rather than *do the shopping*), but the actions become domestic (*walk the dog, Pew tells me a story*), as does the vocabulary (*more tea*). The two structures, imperative and non-past, and the two styles, naval and domestic, end in cosiness, an implicit security in a simple routine with storytelling before bed.

3 Literary Exercise

In the following extract, which is from the beginning of a radio play, identify the non-past verb forms. Say whether they are indicating past, present or future time-settings. Is there anything unusual about them?

Voice 1. I am having a very nice time.

The weather is up and down, but surprisingly warm, on the whole, more often than not.

I hope you're feeling well, and not as peaky as you did, the last time I saw you.

No, you didn't feel peaky, you felt perfectly well, you simply looked peaky.

Do you miss me?

I am having a very nice time and I hope you are glad of that.

At the moment I am dead drunk.

I had five pints in The Fishmongers Arms tonight, followed by three double scotches, and literally rolled home.

When I say home I can assure you that my room is extremely pleasant. So is the bathroom. Extremely pleasant. I have some very pleasant baths indeed in the bathroom. So does everybody else in the house. They all lie quite naked in the bath and have very pleasant baths indeed. All the people in the house go about saying what a superb bath and bathroom the one we share is, they go about telling literally everyone they meet what lovely baths you can get in this place, more or less unparalleled, to put it bluntly.

It's got a lot to do with the landlady, who is a Mrs Withers, a person who turns out to be an utterly charming person of impeccable credentials.

When I said I was drunk I was of course making a joke.

I bet you laughed.

Mother?

Did you get the joke? You know I never touch alcohol.

I like being in this enormous city, all by myself. I expect to make friends in the not too distant future.

I expect to make girlfriends too.

I expect to meet a very nice girl. Having met her, I shall bring her home to meet my mother.

I like walking in this enormous city, all by myself. It's fun to know no-one at all. When I pass people in the street they don't realize that I don't know them from Adam. They know other people and even more other people know them, so they naturally think that even if I don't know them I know the other people. So they look at me, they try to catch my eye, they expect me to speak. But as I do not know them I do not speak. Nor do I ever feel the slightest temptation to do so.

You see, mother, I am not lonely, because all that has ever happened to me is with me, keeps me company; my childhood, for example, through which you, my mother, and he, my father, guided me.

I get on very well with my landlady, Mrs Withers. She tells me I am her solace. I have a drink with her at lunchtime and another one at teatime and then take her for a couple in the evening at The Fishmongers Arms.

Harold Pinter, 1981, *Family Voices*.

In the following finite Verb Phrases, verbs marked for the non-past are in mauve. Verb Phrases consisting of finite auxiliary verbs plus non-finite –ing forms are marked orange, finite auxiliary verbs plus non-finite -ed forms are marked red, and finite auxiliary verbs plus non-finite base forms are marked blue. My comment on the time-setting is expressed in green.

Voice 1. I am having a very nice time. (at the present moment and in the recent past)

The weather is up and down (at the present moment and in the recent past), but surprisingly warm, on the whole, more often than not.

I hope (right now) you're feeling well (right now, and over the last few days), and not as peaky as you did, the last time I saw you.

No, you didn't feel peaky, you felt perfectly well, you simply looked peaky.

Do you miss me? (at the present moment and in the recent past)

I am having a very nice time (at the present moment and in the recent past) and I hope (right now) you are glad of that (right now).

At the moment I am dead drunk (right now).

I had five pints in The Fishmongers Arms tonight, followed by three double scotches, and literally rolled home.

When I say (right now) home I can assure you (right now) that my room is extremely pleasant (at the present moment, in the past, in the future). So is the bathroom (at the present moment, in the past, in the future). Extremely pleasant. I have some very pleasant baths indeed (in the fairly recent past, and in the future, though not right now) in the bathroom. So does everybody else (in the past) in the house. They all lie quite naked in the bath (in the past) and have very pleasant baths indeed (in the past, probably in the future). All the people in the house go about (in the past, probably in the future) saying what a superb bath and bathroom the one we share is (at the present moment, in the past, in the future), they go about (in the past, probably in the future) telling literally everyone they meet (in the past, in the future) what lovely baths you can get (at the present moment, in the past, in the future) in this place, more or less unparalleled, to put it bluntly.

It's got a lot to do with the landlady (at the present moment, in the past, in the future), who is a Mrs Withers (at the present moment, in the past, in the future), a person who turns out to be an utterly charming person of impeccable credentials (at the present moment, in the past, in the future).

When I said I was drunk I was of course making a joke.

I bet you laughed.

Mother?

Did you get the joke? You know (past, present, future) I never touch alcohol (past, present, future).

I like being in this enormous city (recent past, present, future), all by myself. I expect (right now) to make friends in the not too distant future.

I expect (right now) to make girlfriends too.

I expect (right now) to meet a very nice girl. Having met her, I shall bring her home to meet my mother (present declaration of future intent).

I like walking in this enormous city (in the recent past, right now (that is, I like the *idea* of walking right now)), all by myself. It's fun (in the recent past, in the future) to know no-one at all. When I pass people in the street (in the recent past) they don't realize (in the recent past) that I don't know them (in the recent past) from Adam. They know other people (in the recent past) and even more other people know them (in the recent past), so they naturally think (in the recent past) that even if I don't know them (in the recent past) I know the other people (in the recent past). So they look at me (in the recent past), they try to catch my eye (in the recent past), they expect me to speak (in the recent past). But as I do not know them (in the recent past) I do not speak (in the recent past). Nor do I ever feel (in the recent past) the slightest temptation to do so.

You see, mother (right now), I am not lonely (now), because all that has ever happened to me (in the past) is with me (now and in the future), keeps me company (now and in the future); my childhood, for example, through which you, my mother, and he, my father, guided me.

I get on very well with my landlady (past, present, future), Mrs Withers. She tells me (in the recent past) I am her solace (in the recent past). I have a drink with her at lunchtime (in the recent past) and another one at teatime and then take her (in the recent past) for a couple in the evening at The Fishmongers Arms.

Analysis

There are several reasons why this monologue sounds slightly odd (it turns out later to be a letter – this is the start of the play – though at this stage it could be one side of a phone conversation), but non-past usage is not one of them. You may find your interpretations of the time-settings are slightly different from mine, but you'll see that there is a range of time-settings conveyed by the non-past. None are particularly unusual and they don't pose any processing problems for the listener – it's the kind of thing we do with the non-past in conversation all the time. They provide a semblance of normality; a person reflecting on his recent activities.

Commentary

What is unusual is the pragmatics (pragmatics is the name for how language is used to generate meaning in context, the conventions for what is appropriate): to be quite so precise about one's expectations (to meet friends, girls, a very nice girl, a potential wife) with no specific prospect – no bird in the hand; to be quite so emphatic and repetitious about the loveliness of bathing in the rooming-house (although certainly bathrooms in British rooming-houses could be quite appalling); to be quite so specific about the thoughts and intentions of unknown passers-by in the city. The declaration about being drunk, although retracted, could at this point in the play be a plausible explanation.

4 Teaching Point

This section introduces tense: past and non-past; *-ed*, *-s*, and zero markers, and the concept of finite verbs, which are marked for tense. The present tense doesn't necessarily convey a present time-setting; speakers use it to express a range of more-or-less-distant points in time. Switching between past and non-past is not unusual, regardless of the time-setting.

8 Phrasal Verbs

1 Definition of term *Phrasal Verbs*

Prepositions can sit after certain verbs, and are known as Phrasal Verbs:

to sit through, to dig in, to dig around, to rifle through, to cough up, to drag down, to pile in, to sit out, to chip in, to make up, to buy out, to butter up

Phrasal verbs are often conversational in tone. Consider the register (formal/neutral/informal) of:

to do (someone) over, to do (someone) in, to kick off 'to create a fuss, to fight', to turn round and say 'to respond', to have it away with, to have it off with, to have it out with, to get on with, to get off with, to get off on, to put up with

Phrasal verbs correlate more with speech than writing. They vary from dialect to dialect, and you may not have some of the following in your own idiolect [*idiolect*: the speech of an individual]:

Delilah's gone	to the pub
	up the pub
	down the pub
	over the pub
	round the pub

Many of the phrasal verbs in use today are relatively new in the system, and more are being coined – the *Oxford English Dictionary* has no attestations as yet of *to kick off* 'to quarrel, start to make a fuss' [*Oxford English Dictionary* kick, v.[1] phrasal verbs to kick off 'to give the first kick in a football game']. To *kick off* in this sense is synonymous with to *start*, as in "Don't you start!" meaning to complain, criticize, carp [*Oxford English Dictionary* start, v. P3.b.]. However 'relatively new' means within the last six hundred years or so. The verb *doff* is a coalesced form of the phrasal verb to *do off*, first attested in a document dated before 1375, and its sibling *don* is a coalesced form of to *do on*. *Doff* and *don* sound archaic but they are early examples of a construction which is gaining more and more members – linguists say a *type* which is gaining more and more *tokens*. A twenty-first century text is more likely to contain phrasal verbs than a fourteenth-century one.

Phrasal verbs can be divided into two groups, those which are transparent semantically (*to speak out, to jump up*), and those where the sum of the two (or more) elements does not add up to the meaning.

> I can't put up with this any longer

In this case, the semantics of *put* plus *up* plus *with* do not equal 'tolerate'; the baby or foreign learner just has to learn this sequence off by heart. We have to commit the meaning of such sequences to memory, it can't be worked out from the semantics of the elements.

2 Demonstration of Phrasal Verbs

In the following text, the phrasal verbs are marked in orange:

... I had the devils own job to get it out of him though I liked him for that it showed he could hold in and wasnt to be got for the asking he was on the pop of asking me too the night in the kitchen I was rolling the potato cake theres something I want to say to you only for I put him off letting on I was in a temper with my hands and arms full of pasty flour in any case I let out too much the night before talking of dreams so I didnt want to let him know more than was good for him she used to be always embracing me Josie whenever he was there meaning him of course glauming me over and when I said I washed up and down as far as possible asking me did you wash possible the women are always egging on to that putting it on thick when hes there they know by his sly eye blinking a bit putting on the indifferent when they come out with something ...

James Joyce, 1922, *Ulysses*

In the context of this text, the thoughts of the character Molly Bloom, the phrasal verbs could be paraphrased as follows, with the base form of the verb in orange and the postposed prepositions in blue:

to get something out of someone: to force someone to reveal something
to hold in: to remain impervious, stand firm
to get for the asking: to be easily won
to be on the pop of: to be about to
to put someone off: to deter someone
to let on: to pretend

to *let out*: to reveal
to *glaum* someone *over*: to maul (Scots-Irish dialect)
to *wash up/down:* to wash up and down the body
to *egg on to*: to incite, urge, encourage
to *put* it *on* thick: to exaggerate
to *put on* the indifferent: to assume, pretend, dissemble
to *come out with*: to say

We are listening to Molly's memories at this point, and her tone is colloquial and informal. This is largely conveyed by the phrasal verbs.

3 Literary Exercise

Here is Philip Larkin's poem *Mr Bleaney*. Find the phrasal verbs. What do they add to the tone of the poem?

> Mr Bleaney
> 'This was Mr Bleaney's room. He stayed
> The whole time he was at the Bodies, till
> They moved him.' Flowered curtains, thin and frayed,
> Fall to within five inches of the sill,
>
> Whose window shows a strip of building land,
> Tussocky, littered. 'Mr Bleaney took
> My bit of garden properly in hand.'
> Bed, upright chair, sixty-watt bulb, no hook
>
> Behind the door, no room for books or bags –
> 'I'll take it.' So it happens that I lie
> Where Mr Bleaney lay, and stub my fags
> On the same saucer-souvenir, and try
>
> Stuffing my ears with cotton-wool, to drown
> The jabbering set he egged her on to buy.
> I know his habits – what time he came down,
> His preference for sauce to gravy, why
>
> He kept on plugging at the four aways –
> Likewise their yearly frame: the Frinton folk
> Who put him up for summer holidays,
> And Christmas at his sister's house in Stoke.

But if he stood and watched the frigid wind
Tousling the clouds, lay on the fusty bed
Telling himself that this was home, and grinned,
And shivered, without shaking off the dread

That how we live measures our own nature,
And at his age having no more to show
Than one hired box should make him pretty sure
He warranted no better, I don't know.

Philip Larkin, 1955, *Mr Bleaney*

Analysis

The phrasal verbs are:

To be at: 'he was at the Bodies' (perhaps a car body manufactory)
Paraphrase: 'to work at, be employed at'
To fall to: 'Flowered curtains, thin and frayed, / Fall to within five inches of the sill'
Paraphase: 'reach to'
To take in hand: 'Mr Bleaney took / My bit of garden properly in hand.'
Paraphrase: 'to assume responsibility for'
To stub on: 'stub my fags / On the same saucer-souvenir'
Paraphrase, 'to put out, grind out'
To stuff with: 'Stuffing my ears with cotton-wool'
Paraphrase, 'to push in, force in'
To egg on: 'he egged her on' (in reference to a too-loud radio, called a wireless set at the time)
Paraphrase: 'to encourage, exhort'
To come down: 'what time he came down'
Paraphrase: 'to present oneself to the rest of the household in the morning, dressed, washed and shaved, though probably not breakfasted'
To keep on: 'He kept on plugging at the four aways –'
Paraphrase: 'to continue'
To plug at: (in reference to playing the football pools, which he clearly never won much money at)
Paraphrase: 'to repeatedly attempt in the face of failure'
To put up: 'the Frinton folk / Who put him up for summer holidays'
Paraphrase: 'to have as a guest'

To lie on: 'lay on the fusty bed' – here the addition of the preposition doesn't change the core meaning; 'to lie on, under, across, etc.' all mean to lie supine, or prone. Compare *to stuff with, to keep on*, which also retain the primary sense of the verb, in contrast with *to plug at*, which has nothing to do with the primary sense of the word *plug*. *Plug at* is a phrasal verb, whereas the other three can be described as [V + Prep] – the distinction is more fuzzy.

Commentary

The poem has a conversation playing in the background, a conversation between the landlady showing the room and her prospective tenant viewing it. We hear snatches of the landlady's voice but not the tenant's responses to her, apart from "I'll take it.". However, indirectly, we hear her remarks about the habits of her former lodger, so we can infer not only the present conversation between them at the start of the poem, but also, in stanzas 4 and 5, subsequent conversations.

The phrasal verbs occur before the last two stanzas, creating a change in tone at this point: the habitual and physical things that the tenant has learnt about Mr Bleaney, as opposed to the internal and psychological things that the tenant does not know about Mr Bleaney.

This poem was enormously popular at the time of publication, and has proved to be one of Larkin's most famous works. It may have to do with the readership identifying with the tenant – after the Second World War many people lived in lodgings rather than owned their own property. The non-attainment of youthful ambition becomes a concern in middle age.

4 Teaching Point

Being relatively new in the system, phrasal verbs will often sound conversational and informal in register. They lend a casual, everyday tone to a discourse.

9 Auxiliary Verbs

1 Definition of term *Auxiliary Verbs*

Certain verbs can cluster together, in which case the first one will be the finite auxiliary verb (finite verbs are marked for person, number and tense) and the second, third, fourth and fifth will be *–ed*, *–ing* or base forms. In the following examples I have taken the main, or lexical, verb *whistle* and preceded it with various combinations of auxiliaries. I have marked the finite auxiliary verb in lilac, the *–ed* forms in blue, the *–ing* forms in green, and the base forms in pink. (Note that *-ed* forms aren't always marked with *–ed*, they can change their stem vowel instead.)

> I am whistling
> I have whistled
> I would have whistled
> I could have been whistling
> I might have been being whistled at
> I did not whistle
> the tune was whistled by me

Auxiliary verbs are those verbs which can sit between the pronoun *I* and the final word in the sequence, the main lexical (or meaning-carrying) verb. The whole sequence of verbs is known as the Verb Phrase. Auxiliaries mostly consist of the forms of the verbs *be, have, do*, and what are known as the *modal* verbs (modal auxiliary verbs are discussed in Chapter 11; there are nine central modals: *would, will, should, shall, could, can, may, might, must*). The word *auxiliary* ultimately comes from the Latin word *auxilium*, meaning 'help', and auxiliary verbs help the main or lexical verb by doing its tense-work: contrast *I am whistling* with *I was whistling*.

The last Verb Phrase in the sequence above, was whistled, is known as the *passive*. The passive almost always consists of part of the verb 'to be' plus an *–ed* form. It can lack an agent: *the tune was whistled*, or the agent can sit in a Prepositional Phrase: [*by me*]. As the [*by* + agent] is optional, passives are useful for authors wishing to elide the agent of an action.

Auxiliary verbs are small frequent particles and their presence in literary texts is to be expected – as you see, they can stack up. Restriction to one type of construction alone, or their absence altogether, is more likely to warrant comment than a mixture of combinations.

2 Demonstration of term *auxiliary verbs*

Read through the following text, looking out for the auxiliary verbs *have, be, do,* and any modal auxiliaries.

When I was bathed and in pyjamas and dressing-gown by the imitation logs that glowed so rosily on the hearth in my room, I said: 'Mummy, who will have Mr Mellon's snuff-boxes when he dies?'
　My mother frowned a little.
　'We don't want to think about people dying.'
　'But I want to know,' I persisted.
　My mother seemed to be wondering whether to tell me something or not.
　'Has Phyllis explained that Mr Mellon is going to adopt her?' she asked, lifting her eyebrows.
　'No, Phyllis says hardly anything at all.' Then the full meaning of my mother's words came to me and I added excitedly, 'Will *she* have the snuff-boxes and everything then?'
　'I expect so, darling, but it won't be for a long time, so don't talk about it or think about it any more.'
　But once in bed, with the lights out, I thought of nothing else. It seemed to me the greatest waste that Phyllis should have anything more than the necessities of life; then my imagination was caught by the wonderful change in her fortunes; for, without having heard a word on the subject, I pictured Mrs Slade and Phyllis in very difficult circumstances before they had come to Mr Mellon.
　I must have been asleep for some hours when I was woken by soft bumping sounds and the murmur of voices. The noises frightened me and even after I had recognized one of the voices as Mrs Slade's, I felt anxious. What could be happening? There was another gentle bump. Mrs Slade said: 'There we are! Up at last!' and I heard a sort of comfortable grunt from Mr Mellon.
　I realized that she was wheeling him to bed. Could she have pulled him up the stairs alone? The stairs were shallow, but Mr Mellon would be very heavy and awkward in his wheel-chair. It did not seem possible for so small a woman.

Denton Welch, 1948, *The Trout Stream*

Here is the text again with finite auxiliary verbs in lilac, *–ed* forms in blue, *–ing* forms in green, and base forms in pink.

When I was bathed and in pyjamas and dressing-gown by the imitation logs that glowed so rosily on the hearth in my room, I said: 'Mummy, who will have Mr Mellon's snuff-boxes when he dies?'

My mother frowned a little.

'We don't want to think about people dying.'

'But I want to know,' I persisted.

My mother seemed to be wondering whether to tell me something or not.

'Has Phyllis explained that Mr Mellon is going to adopt her?' she asked, lifting her eyebrows.

'No, Phyllis says hardly anything at all.' Then the full meaning of my mother's words came to me and I added excitedly, 'Will she have the snuff-boxes and everything then?'

'I expect so, darling, but it won't be for a long time, so don't talk about it or think about it any more.'

But once in bed, with the lights out, I thought of nothing else. It seemed to me the greatest waste that Phyllis should have anything more than the necessities of life; then my imagination was caught by the wonderful change in her fortunes; for, without having heard a word on the subject, I pictured Mrs Slade and Phyllis in very difficult circumstances before they had come to Mr Mellon.

I must have been asleep for some hours when I was woken by soft bumping sounds and the murmur of voices. The noises frightened me and even after I had recognized one of the voices as Mrs Slade's, I felt anxious. What could be happening? There was another gentle bump. Mrs Slade said: 'There we are! Up at last!' and I heard a sort of comfortable grunt from Mr Mellon.

I realized that she was wheeling him to bed. Could she have pulled him up the stairs alone? The stairs were shallow, but Mr Mellon would be very heavy and awkward in his wheel-chair. It did not seem possible for so small a woman.

Not all *–ed, -ing* and base forms are preceded by an auxiliary verb:

the imitation logs that glowed – contrast *glowed* with *were glowing*: *glowed* is a simple, one-element, past tense verb here.

We don't want to think about people dying – the Verb Phrase consists of [auxiliary *do* + base form *want*], followed by [preposition *to* + base form *think*]. What about *dying*? This sits in a separate clause, and is known as a non-finite *–ing* clause (more on *–ing* forms in Chapter 18). There is no finite auxiliary verb sitting between *people* and *dying*. It could be paraphrased as

We don't want to think about people who are dying, where the Verb Phrase *are dying* consists of [auxiliary *be* + *-ing*].

My mother seemed to be wondering – some quasi-auxiliaries exist, quasi in the sense that they consist of a small cluster of words rather than a single verb. Here, [*seemed*] is the finite verb marked for person, number and tense, followed by [preposition *to* + base form + *-ing* form]. If you had analysed [*seemed to be wondering*] as an auxiliary followed by a base form and an *–ing* form, you would not be incorrect.

without having heard a word – again, there is no finite auxiliary present. In context, it could be paraphrased as *without my having heard a word*, and the possessive pronoun *my* tells us that a noun construction will follow.

soft bumping sounds – *-ing* forms can act as adjectives premodifying nouns, as here with *bumping*.

Despite the various combinations of auxiliary verbs with *–ed, -ing* and base forms, this text is not hard to process and speakers have no trouble at all in putting their auxiliary verbs in sequence.

3 Literary Exercise

Identify the auxiliary verbs in the following text.

Coming out from a lecture one evening, she said, they had found torrential rain, and Simon was the kind of man who never – in England, anyhow – went anywhere without an umbrella and a folded plastic raincoat.

Under the umbrella they had bolted towards the tube station – he and Martha splashing through puddles, past closed shops and open pubs.

"*I* got the umbrella, not Miss Smarty-boots. We sat in the train, dripping and steaming and shivering, and he put questions to me about the lecture that he'd been too shy to ask in front of the others. I realized that he knew a great, great deal more than I had imagined."

The beef olives had been eaten, without, it seemed, making much impression. A pudding that followed was also a matter of indifference.

"He got off at Swiss Cottage," Martha said. "After that we always went home together, whether it rained or not."

She finished her pudding, absent-mindedly helped herself to more, and said, "I was starving." After all that messing about Amy found this difficult to understand.

"One night we went to a pub, and the next week I asked him back to my room. We were slow movers. Do you know it was only the second time he had had sex with anyone, and he is twenty-seven. So sad. Wasn't all that good at it, but neither am I. I only do it because I feel sorry for them."

"Some more pudding?"

"No, I don't believe I will."

Elizabeth Taylor, 1976, *Blaming*

Culinary note: *Oxford English Dictionary* olive, *n.1* and *adj*. A. I. 5. beef olives 'A dish made from slices of beef or veal, typically rolled around a filling of onions and herbs, stewed, and served in gravy.'

Here is the text again with finite auxiliary verbs in lilac, *–ed* forms in blue, *–ing* forms in green, and base forms in pink.

Coming out from a lecture one evening, she said, they had found torrential rain, and Simon was the kind of man who never – in England, anyhow – went anywhere without an umbrella and a folded plastic raincoat.

Under the umbrella they had bolted towards the tube station – he and Martha splashing through puddles, past closed shops and open pubs.

"*I* got the umbrella, not Miss Smarty-boots. We sat in the train, dripping and steaming and shivering, and he put questions to me about the lecture that he'd been too shy to ask in front of the others. I realized that he knew a great, great deal more than I had imagined."

The beef olives had been eaten, without, it seemed, making much impression. A pudding that followed was also a matter of indifference.

"He got off at Swiss Cottage," Martha said. "After that we always went home together, whether it rained or not."

She finished her pudding, absent-mindedly helped herself to more, and said, "I was starving." After all that messing about Amy found this difficult to understand.

"One night we went to a pub, and the next week I asked him back to my room. We were slow movers. Do you know it was only the second time he had had sex with anyone, and he is twenty-seven. So sad. Wasn't all that good at it, but neither am I. I only do it because I feel sorry for them."

"Some more pudding?"

"No, I don't believe I will."

Analysis

Coming out from a lecture – the auxiliary is elided: *As they were coming out from a lecture one evening*...

he and Martha splashing through puddles – the auxiliary verb is elided: *were* or *had been splashing* through puddles

past closed shops – just like *–ing* forms, *–ed* forms can act as adjectives premodifying nouns: *closed* premodifies *shops*.

We sat in the train, dripping and steaming and shivering – there are two clauses here, [*we sat in the train*], and then an elided conjunction and auxiliary: [*and we were dripping and steaming and shivering*]

Commentary

This extract is a past-tense narration about a meal shared between Martha and Amy at which Martha recalls and relates events set further back in the past, when she met Simon. The Verb Phrases with auxiliary *be* and *do* (*was starving, do you know*) indicate the here-and-now timeframe of the meal, whereas the Verb Phrases with auxiliary *have* (*had found, had bolted, 'd been, had imagined, had had*) indicate a more distant past when Simon and Martha first got together. The exception is the three-element stack, *the beef olives had been eaten* ('by Martha' is implicit). This is a passive usage which could have been expressed actively: *Martha had eaten the beef olives.* Martha has been so intent on her narrative that she has failed to notice or praise her dinner, thereby annoying Amy, who regards Martha's discourse as 'all that messing about'. The passive enables the author to distance Martha from the act of eating and instead foreground her speech, even though whilst talking Martha has eaten all of her dinner and two puddings, seemingly without gratitude.

4 Teaching Point

Auxiliaries are small and frequent and easily overlooked – but anything expressed passively could have been expressed actively, so question the effect.

If you have learnt a foreign language you may be wondering why terminology such as *imperfect* and *pluperfect* is not used. There are several reasons. Such terminology was not invented for describing English, and does not always fit the English language very well. Nouns and verbs are often fuzzy in use. Speakers don't actually speak in sentences much of the time, and using a term like *imperfect* would commit you as having analysed a sequence as a Verb Phrase, whereas in reality it might be ambiguous. *-ed* forms and *–ing* forms are transparent terms; you don't have to remember what they mean as they show you.

10 Auxiliary Verb *do*

1 Definition of term auxiliary verb *do*

Do is one of the most frequent verbs in English. Yet it started life as a relatively low-frequency lexical verb meaning 'to cause, make happen':

Old English
doþ þæt þæt folc sitte
do   that the folk sit
'make the people sit'

Before 1400 *do* was hardly used as an auxiliary verb. After 1400 it began to be used as an auxiliary, until in the century 1500–1600 it was used in all the following syntactic slots:

	Affirmative	Negative
Declaratives:	Ellinthorpe doth denye it	she doth not declare
Questions:	how do you do?	dont you know?
Imperatives:	do you sit here	dont be afraid

Then, after a heyday in the late 1500s-early 1600s, *do*-usage began to retreat, until the present-day distribution was reached around 1700, whereby we use auxiliary *do* in affirmative and negative questions: (Did you go? Didn't you go?), negative imperatives (Don't go!), and negative declaratives (You don't often go); but not affirmative imperatives (Go! rather than *Do go! (unless we are being emphatic or super-polite, in which case, do sit down, do have another scone)), nor in affirmative declaratives (we only say they do go in Standard English when being emphatic).

    Do also became used as a pro-verb. Pro-verbs are used to avoid repeating a verb already mentioned: I love sunshine, as do all sun-starved northerners, where *do* stands in for 'love sunshine' (try repositioning it: *as all sun-starved northerners love sunshine*).

    So in present-day Standard English, *do* can act as a lexical verb meaning 'to act', as an auxiliary verb in negative declaratives, questions, and negative imperatives, and as a pro-verb. Quite why it leapt out of its lexical slot into its auxiliary role and then retreated from affirmative declaratives and imperatives is not fully understood. *Do* is one of those small, frequent grammatical devices that usually escapes notice due to being so very commonplace. Which is why it's worth becoming sensitivised to dense patches of *do*: why did the author place them there?

2 Demonstration of auxiliary verb *do*

I said, 'Who knows?'

He said, 'Nobody. Well... Nobody.'

I said, 'So that means half the golf club knows. Have you taken her there? Where have you taken her? Who's seen her? Am I a complete blummin' laughing stock?'

He said, 'No. That's not it at all. There isn't nobody, Ba. I swear to God. It's me. It's my stuff. I've got shoes and undies and everything. You're the best wife in the world. I just like dressing up. It don't mean there's anything wrong with you. If there's anything wrong with anybody, it's me. Only I don't do anybody any harm. A lot of men do it, Ba. You might not realize it, but a lot of men do it. It's only like... like an interest.'

An *interest*. He's got a red crystal pleat two-piece in his cupboard, and things I haven't even seen that he wants to wear. I've known him since the day we started school. We've got grandchildren, and a daughter who's marrying a solicitor, and he's trying to make out it's an *interest*.

Cactuses are an interest. Or badminton.

I said, 'Have you seen a doctor?'

He said, 'It's not like that.'

I said, 'No, you're right. It's nothing like that. You've been caught buying your fancy woman presents, and all you can do is try to wriggle out of it, pretending to be a pervert. I've heard of some stunts in my time, but this one beats them all.' I said, 'Why can't you just own up? Be a man? Let's get it over and done with.'

He said, 'That's about the size of it, isn't it? You'd be happier about it if I'd got another woman. You'd sooner be married to a cheating bastard than somebody who just wants to wear a frock every now and then and not do nobody no harm. Eh? Is that it?'

I don't know. How should I know? We were all right till Jason brought that bridesmaid's dress round. We were happy as Larry. He says he was just waiting till after the wedding before he told me, but he wasn't. He knew I don't want to hear stuff like that.

He said, 'I'll sleep in Jason's old room tonight.'

He said, 'You think something like this'll fade away as you get older. You think you'll stop wanting to do it, but you don't. And then fifty comes. You get to fifty and you think, if there's something you want to do, you'd better get on and do it.'

He said, 'I love you, Ba. If I could have carried on without you having to know I would have done.'

He didn't though, did he?

Laurie Graham, 1998, *The Dress Circle*

It don't mean	negative declarative auxiliary verb (regional dialect – Standard English *It doesn't mean*)
I don't do anybody any harm	negative declarative auxiliary verb, base form lexical verb (original Old English sense, 'to cause')
A lot of men do it	third-person plural, present-tense, lexical verb
all you can do	base form, lexical verb
Let's get it over and done with	*-ed* form (past participle), lexical verb
and not do nobody no harm	base form, lexical verb (original Old English sense, 'to cause')
I don't know	negative declarative auxiliary verb
I don't want to hear	negative declarative auxiliary verb
you'll stop wanting to do it	base form, lexical verb
but you don't	pro-verb, standing for 'stop wanting to'.
there's something you want to do	base form, lexical verb
get on and do it	base form, lexical verb
I would have done	*-ed* form (past participle), pro-verb, standing for 'carried on'
He didn't though	negative declarative auxiliary verb, past tense, pro-verb, standing for 'carried on without you having to know'
did he?	tag question, past tense

This is the moment when Ba realises that Bobs, her husband of more than two decades, dresses in women's clothing. (Ba and Bobs live in the hinterland of Birmingham and the story is written in Ba's first-person Midlands dialect.) Although the analysis shows that there's a considerable and versatile amount of *do*-use, it is not striking, unusual or otherwise remarkable. *Do* is highly useful when something embarrassing or difficult needs to be articulated. Only on one occasion does Bobs state *to wear a frock*; otherwise he says *dressing up, a lot of men do it, an interest, something like this, you'll stop wanting to do it, something you want to do, get on and do it*. The taboo explicit form ("dressing like a woman") is euphemized as *dressing up/it/an interest/something*. *Do* facilitates this evasion by enabling elision and omission.

Fashion note: crystal pleat is a tiny accordion pleat used on evening-wear fabric like chiffon.

3 Literary Exercise

Locate and analyse the uses of *do* – and pay attention to omission of expected *do* in the following text. What is the tone of this passage and how does *do* – or lack of *do* – help create it?

When one comes to think of it, few bicycles do realize the poster. On only one poster that I can recollect have I seen the rider represented as doing any work. But then this man was being pursued by a bull. In ordinary cases the object of the artist is to convince the hesitating neophyte that the sport of bicycling consists in sitting8 on a luxurious saddle, and being moved rapidly in the direction you wish to go by unseen heavenly powers.

    Generally speaking, the rider is a lady, and then one feels that, for perfect bodily rest combined with entire freedom from mental anxiety, slumber upon a water-bed cannot compare with bicycle-riding upon a hilly road. No fairy travelling on a summer cloud could take things more easily than does the bicycle-girl, according to the poster. Her costume for cycling in hot weather is ideal. Old-fashioned landladies might refuse her lunch, it is true; and a narrow-minded police force might desire to secure her, and wrap her in a rug preliminary to summoning her. But such she heeds not. Uphill and downhill, through traffic that might tax the ingenuity of a cat, over road surfaces calculated to break the average steam-roller she passes, a vision of idle loveliness; her fair hair streaming to the wind, her sylph-like form poised airily, one foot upon the saddle, the other resting lightly upon the lamp. Sometimes she condescends to sit down on the saddle; then she puts her feet on the rests, lights a cigarette, and waves above her head a Chinese lantern.

    Less often, it is a mere male thing that rides the machine. He is not so accomplished an acrobat as is the lady; but simple tricks such as standing on the saddle and waving flags, drinking beer or beef-tea while riding, he can and does perform. Something, one supposes, he must do to occupy his mind: sitting still hour after hour on this machine, having no work to do, nothing to think about, must pall upon any man of active temperament. Thus it is that we see him riding on his pedals as he nears the top of some high hill to apostrophize the sun, or address poetry to the surrounding scenery.

Jerome K. Jerome, 1900, *Three Men on the Bummel*

Analysis

few bicycles do realize the poster	affirmative declarative auxiliary verb, emphatic
represented as doing any work	-*ing* form, lexical verb
could take things more easily than does the bicycle-girl	pro-verb, standing for 'takes things'
he can and does perform	affirmative declarative auxiliary verb, emphatic
he must do	base form, lexical verb
no work to do	base form, lexical verb

Commentary

The tone of the text is humorous. The humour comes from the high-flown classical style used to describe the tricks. Notice, for example, the delayed verb ("Uphill and downhill, through traffic … over road surfaces … she passes"), premodification in the Noun Phrase ("her sylph-like form"), classical rhetoric ("to apostrophize the sun"– *apostrophe* is a technical rhetorical term for an exclamatory address) – and lack of auxiliary *do* where it is required today: "But such she heeds not", rather than 'But she does not heed', giving an old-fashioned, quasi-Biblical tone. Affirmative declarative *do* provides bathos (*bathos*: from the elevated to the commonplace): "drinking beer or beef-tea while riding, he can and does perform"; rather than 'while riding he performs drinking beer or beef-tea'.

4 Teaching Point

Do may seem unworthy of a literary critic's attention, and in many texts it will have no particular literary significance. But because it does so much syntactic work, it can be a useful tool for present-day authors, and you need to be aware of its changing uses when reading older literature.

11 Modal Auxiliary Verbs

1 Definition of term *modal auxiliary verbs*

There are nine central modal auxiliary verbs: *shall, should, can, could, will, would, may, must, might*. There are also quasi-modal auxiliary verbs: *ought to, need to, has to*. Why only quasi? Because the nine modals sit before the base form: *I shall go, I could go*, etc., but with *ought/need/has* a *to* has to be inserted: *I ought to go, it needs to be done, it has to be zero degrees* (said in an icy wind).

The modal auxiliaries' job is to express possibility (hypothesis, futurity, doubt) and necessity (by inference, such-and-such must necessarily be the case); that is, matters beyond the factual here and now. This is known as the *irrealis*. As we spend much time thinking and talking about the irrealis, modal auxiliaries are very common.

A further distinction is to be made between epistemic and deontic modals, which distinguish between possibility one the one hand and obligation on the other. Consider the following: "the importance of time and patience cannot be underestimated". *Cannot* is used in its deontic (obligation) sense, meaning that we must not underestimate the importance of time and patience. But consider "the importance of time and patience cannot be overestimated". Here, *cannot* is used in its epistemic (possibility) sense, meaning that it is not possible to overestimate the importance of time and patience, that importance being so great.

2 Demonstration of modal auxiliary verbs

In the following extract, Nenna and Maurice are talking about a criminal, Harry, who stores his stolen goods on Maurice's boat, which is also called *Maurice*. Look out for the modal and quasi-modal auxiliaries.

During the small hours, tipsy Maurice became an oracle, ambiguous, wayward, but impressive. Even his voice changed a little. He told the sombre truths of the light-hearted, betraying in a casual hour what was never intended to be shown. If the tide was low the two of them watched the gleams on the foreshore, at half tide they heard the water chuckling, waiting to lift the boats, at flood tide they saw the river as a powerful god, bearded with the white foam of detergents, calling home the twenty-seven lost rivers of London, sighing as the night declined.

'Maurice, ought I to go away?'
'You can't.'

'You said you were going to go away yourself.'

'No-one believed it. You didn't. What do the others think?'

'They think your boat belongs to Harry.'

'Nothing belongs to Harry, certainly all that stuff in the hold doesn't. He finds it easier to live without property. As to *Maurice*, my godmother gave me the money to buy a bit of property when I left Southport.'

'I've never been to Southport.'

'It's very nice. You take the train from the middle of Liverpool, and it's the last station, right out by the seaside.'

'Have you been back since?'

'No.'

'If *Maurice* belongs to you, why do you have to put up with Harry?'

'I can't answer that.'

'What will you do if the police come?'

'What will you do if your husband doesn't?'

Nenna thought, I must take the opportunity to get things settled for me, even if it's only by chance, like throwing straws into the current. She repeated –

'Maurice, what shall I do?'

'Well, have you been to see him yet?'

'Not yet. But of course I ought to. As soon as I can find someone to stay with the girls, for a night or two if it's necessary, I'm going to go. Thank you for making my mind up.'

'No, don't do that.'

'Don't do what?'

'Don't thank me.'

'Why not?'

'Not for that.'

'But, you know, by myself I can't make my mind up.'

'You shouldn't do it at all.'

'Why not, Maurice?'

'Why should you think it's a good thing to do? Why should it make you any happier? There isn't one kind of happiness, there's all kinds. Decision is torment for anyone with imagination. When you decide, you multiply the things you might have done and now never can. If there's even one person who might be hurt by a decision, you should never make it. They tell you, make up your mind or it will be too late, but if it's really too late, we should be grateful. You know very well that we're two of the same kind, Nenna. It's right for us to live where we do, between land and water. You, my dear, you're half in love with your husband, then there's Martha who's half a child and half a girl, Richard who can't give up being half in the Navy, Willis who's half an artist and half a longshoreman, a cat who's half alive and half dead . . .'

He stopped before describing himself, if, indeed, he had been going to do so.

Penelope Fitzgerald, 1979, *Offshore*

Here is the text again, with the modal verbs marked in dark orange and the quasi-modals in light orange.

During the small hours, tipsy Maurice became an oracle, ambiguous, wayward, but impressive. Even his voice changed a little. He told the sombre truths of the lighthearted, betraying in a casual hour what was never intended to be shown. If the tide was low the two of them watched the gleams on the foreshore, at half tide they heard the water chuckling, waiting to lift the boats, at flood tide they saw the river as a powerful god, bearded with the white foam of detergents, calling home the twenty-seven lost rivers of London, sighing as the night declined.

'Maurice, ought I to go away?'

'You can't.'

'You said you were going to go away yourself.'

'No-one believed it. You didn't. What do the others think?'

'They think your boat belongs to Harry.'

'Nothing belongs to Harry, certainly all that stuff in the hold doesn't. He finds it easier to live without property. As to *Maurice*, my godmother gave me the money to buy a bit of property when I left Southport.'

'I've never been to Southport.'

'It's very nice. You take the train from the middle of Liverpool, and it's the last station, right out by the seaside.'

'Have you been back since?'

'No.'

'If *Maurice* belongs to you, why do you have to put up with Harry?'

'I can't answer that.'

'What will you do if the police come?'

What will you do if your husband doesn't?'

Nenna thought, I must take the opportunity to get things settled for me, even if it's only by chance, like throwing straws into the current. She repeated –

'Maurice, what shall I do?'

'Well, have you been to see him yet?'

'Not yet. But of course I ought to. As soon as I can find someone to stay with the girls, for a night or two if it's necessary, I'm going to go. Thank you for making my mind up.'

'No, don't do that.'
'Don't do what?'
'Don't thank me.'
'Why not?'
'Not for that.'
'But, you know, by myself I can't make my mind up.'
'You shouldn't do it at all.'
'Why not, Maurice?'

'Why should you think it's a good thing to do? Why should it make you any happier? There isn't one kind of happiness, there's all kinds. Decision is torment for anyone with imagination. When you decide, you multiply the things you might have done and now never can. If there's even one person who might be hurt by a decision, you should never make it. They tell you, make up your mind or it will be too late, but if it's really too late, we should be grateful. You know very well that we're two of the same kind, Nenna. It's right for us to live where we do, between land and water. You, my dear, you're half in love with your husband, then there's Martha who's half a child and half a girl, Richard who can't give up being half in the Navy, Willis who's half an artist and half a longshoreman, a cat who's half alive and half dead . . .'

He stopped before describing himself, if, indeed, he had been going to do so.

Nenna and Maurice are indecisive characters, and their inability to make firm and lasting decisions is conveyed by use of modal and quasi-modal auxiliaries (this is a dense concentration of modals for so short a text) and open-ended questions. When considering whether auxiliary *have to* is acting as a modal or not, see if it can be replaced by a modal. In context, *Why do you have to put up with Harry?* can be rewritten as *Why must you put up with Harry?*

Nenna and Maurice's conversation is largely about the irrealis. Concrete facts are not discussed, other than a brief dismissal of Southport. Rather, they consider future actions, and voice opinion about decision-making. Notice the use of deontic and epistemic *can*:

'Maurice, ought I to go away?'
'You can't.'

Is this use of *can* epistemic (possibility): 'you are physically unable to leave your boat, you wouldn't survive on land', or is it deontic (obligation): 'you shouldn't leave because if you do I'll be lonely without you'?

'If *Maurice* belongs to you, why do you have to put up with Harry?'
'I can't answer that.'

Is this epistemic *can* ('I am unable to answer that because I do not know the answer') or deontic *can* ('I have no intention of telling you that')?

> Richard who can't give up being half in the Navy.

Similarly, is Richard unable or unwilling to give up being half in the Navy? These ambiguities are not resolved in the text and it's not clear if either or both the speakers know themselves. Further, the tokens of *should* can be analysed to see if they express possibility, obligation, or whether they are ambiguous:

> If there's even one person who might be hurt by a decision, you should never make it.

This sounds like personal opinion (epistemic), 'I don't think that you ought to make a decision'; 'possibly, you ought not to make a decision'. Contrast it with the next token:

> They tell you, make up your mind or it will be too late, but if it's really too late, we should be grateful.

This sounds more forceful (deontic): 'it's too late, therefore our gratitude is obligatory'.

In literary texts, such ambiguity can be highly useful for authors as it allows multiple interpretations. Here, the overall effect of so many modals and quasi-modals is to keep the discussion in the irrealis, conveying Nenna and Maurice's ineffectual and inconclusive thought-processes.

3 Literary Exercise

The extract below is from a play about estate agents trying to make sales. Levene, an estate agent, is pretending to be D. Ray Morton, an American Express executive and potential buyer, in order that Roma, an estate agent, can evade Lingk, a client. They have set up the codeword *Kenilworth* as a cue to prompt a quick exit. Identify the modal auxiliaries and quasi-modal auxiliaries. Are there any ambiguities?

LINGK. I've got to talk to you...

ROMA. I've got to get Ray to O'Hare... (*To* LEVENE:) Come on, let's hustle... (*Over his shoulder.*) John! Call American Express in *Pittsburgh* for Mr Morton, will you, tell them he's on the one o'clock. (*To* LINGK:) I'll see you ... Christ, I'm sorry you came all the way in ... I'm running Ray over to O'Hare ... You wait here, I'll ... no. (*To* LEVENE:) I'm meeting your man at the Bank ... (*To* LINGK:) I wish you'd phoned ... I'll tell you, wait: (*To* LINGK:) Are you and Jinny going to be home tonight? (*He rubs his forehead.*)

LINGK. I ...

LEVENE. Rick.

ROMA. What?

LEVENE. *Kenilworth ...?*

ROMA. I'm sorry ...?

LEVENE. *Kenilworth.*

ROMA. Oh, God ... Oh, God ... (ROMA *takes* LINGK *aside, sotto:*) Jim, excuse me ... Ray, I told you, who he is is *the* Senior Vice-President American Express. His family owns thirty-two per ... Over the past years I've sold him ... I can't tell you the dollar amount, but *quite* a lot of land. I promised five *weeks* ago that I'd go to the wife's birthday party in Kenilworth tonight. (*He sighs.*) I *have* to go. You understand. They treat me like a member of the family, so I have to go. It's funny, you know, you get a picture of the Corporation Type Company Man, all business ... this man, *no*. We'll go out to his home sometime. Let's see. (*He checks his datebook.*) Tomorrow. No. Tomorrow, I'm in L. A. ... *Monday* ... I'll take you to lunch, where would you like to go?

LINGK. My wife ...

    ROMA *rubs his head.*

LEVENE (*standing in the door*). Rick ...?

ROMA. I'm sorry, Jim. I can't talk now. I'll call you tonight ... I'm sorry. I'm coming, Ray.

    He starts for the door.

LINGK. My wife said I have to cancel the deal.

ROMA. It's a common reaction, Jim. I'll tell you what it is, and I know that that's why you married her. One of the reasons is *prudence*. It's a sizeable investment. One thinks *twice* ... it's also something *women* have. It's just a reaction to the size of the investment. *Monday*, if you'd invite me for dinner again ... (to LEVENE:) This woman can *cook* ...

LEVENE. (*simultaneously*). I'm sure she can ...

ROMA (*to* LINGK). We're going to talk. I'm going to *tell* you something. Because (*Sotto*:) there's something about your acreage I want you to know. I can't talk about it now. I really shouldn't. And, in fact, by *law*, I . . . (*he shrugs, resigned.*) The man next to you, he bought his lot at forty-*two*, he phoned to say that he'd *already* had an offer . . . (ROMA *rubs his head.*)

LEVENE. Rick . . . ?

ROMA. I'm coming, Ray . . . what a day! I'll call you this evening, Jim. I'm sorry you had to come in . . . Monday, lunch.

LINGK. My wife . . .

LEVENE. Rick, we really have to go.

LINGK. My wife . . .

ROMA. Monday.

LINGK. She called the Consumer . . . the Attorney, I don't know. The Attorney Gen . . . they said we have three days . . .

ROMA. *Who* did she call?

LINGK. I don't know, the Attorney Gen . . . the . . . some Consumer office, umm . . .

ROMA. Why did she do *that*, Jim?

LINGK. I don't know. (*Pause.*) They said we have three days. (*Pause.*) They said we have three days.

ROMA. Three days.

LINGK. To . . . you know. (*Pause.*)

ROMA. No I don't know. *Tell* me.

LINGK. To change our minds.

David Mamet, 1984, *Glengarry Glen Ross*

Here is the text again, with the modals and quasi-modals in orange.

LINGK. I've got to talk to you . . .

ROMA. I've got to get Ray to O'Hare . . . (*To* LEVENE:) Come on, let's hustle . . . (*Over his shoulder.*) John! Call American Express in *Pittsburgh* for Mr Morton, will you, tell them he's on the one o'clock. (*To* LINGK:) I'll see you . . . Christ, I'm sorry you came all the way in . . . I'm running Ray over to O'Hare . . . You wait here, I'll . . . no. (*To* LEVENE:) I'm meeting your man at the Bank . . . (*To* LINGK:) I wish you'd phoned . . . I'll tell you, wait: (*To* LINGK:) Are you and Jinny going to be home tonight? (*He rubs his forehead.*)

LINGK. I . . .

LEVENE. Rick.

ROMA. What?

LEVENE. *Kenilworth . . . ?*

ROMA. I'm sorry . . . ?

LEVENE. *Kenilworth.*

ROMA. Oh, God . . . Oh, God . . . (ROMA *takes* LINGK *aside, sotto*:) Jim, excuse me . . . Ray, I told you, who he is is *the* Senior Vice-President American Express. His family owns thirty-two per . . . Over the past years I've sold him . . . I can't tell you the dollar amount, but *quite* a lot of land. I promised five *weeks* ago that I'd go to the wife's birthday party in Kenilworth tonight. (*He sighs.*) I have to go. You understand. They treat me like a member of the family, so I have to go. It's funny, you know, you get a picture of the Corporation Type Company Man, all business . . . this man, *no*. We'll go out to his home sometime. Let's see. (*He checks his datebook.*) Tomorrow. No. Tomorrow, I'm in L. A. . . . *Monday* . . . I'll take you to lunch, where would you like to go?

LINGK. My wife . . .

> ROMA *rubs his head.*

LEVENE (*standing in the door*). Rick . . . ?

ROMA. I'm sorry, Jim. I can't talk now. I'll call you tonight . . . I'm sorry. I'm coming, Ray.

> *He starts for the door.*

LINGK. My wife said I have to cancel the deal.

ROMA. It's a common reaction, Jim. I'll tell you what it is, and I know that that's why you married her. One of the reasons is *prudence*. It's a sizeable investment. One thinks *twice* . . . it's also something *women* have. It's just a reaction to the size of the investment. *Monday*, if you'd invite me for dinner again . . . (to LEVENE:) This woman can *cook* . . .

LEVENE. (*simultaneously*). I'm sure she can . . .

ROMA (*to* LINGK). We're going to talk. I'm going to *tell* you something. Because (*Sotto*:) there's something about your acreage I want you to know. I can't talk about it now. I really shouldn't. And, in fact, by *law*, I ... (*he shrugs, resigned.*) The man next to you, he bought his lot at forty-*two*, he phoned to say that he'd *already* had an offer ... (ROMA *rubs his head.*)

LEVENE. Rick ...?

ROMA. I'm coming, Ray ... what a day! I'll call you this evening, Jim. I'm sorry you had to come in ... Monday, lunch.

LINGK. My wife ...

LEVENE. Rick, we really have to go.

LINGK. My wife ...

ROMA. Monday.

LINGK. She called the Consumer ... the Attorney, I don't know. The Attorney Gen ... they said we have three days ...

ROMA. *Who* did she call?

LINGK. I don't know, the Attorney Gen ... the ... some Consumer office, umm ...

ROMA. Why did she do *that*, Jim?

LINGK. I don't know. (*Pause.*) They said we have three days. (*Pause.*) They said we have three days.

ROMA. Three days.

LINGK. To ... you know. (*Pause.*)

ROMA. No I don't know. *Tell* me.

LINGK. To change our minds.

Analysis

At this point in the play, Roma is blustering. He uses *will/shall* (as they are usually represented on the page as '*ll*, we can't tell which) to talk about imaginary events in the future which he has no intention of fulfilling: meeting Lingk, talking to Lingk, calling Lingk, taking Lingk to lunch, taking Lingk to Ray's house. He uses *have to* to indicate (fictional) social obligation (the two tokens of *I have to go* and *we really have to go* are synonymous with *I/We must go*, unlike *I'm sorry you had to come in*). He exploits the ambiguity of deontic/epistemic *can* in *I can't tell you the dollar amount*, which sounds epistemic, as in 'there are reasons why I'm not telling you', but is really deontic, as in 'I can't tell you because there is no dollar amount, the sale never happened'. He exploits deontic/epistemic *can* and *should* in *there's something about your acreage I want you to know. I can't talk about it now. I really shouldn't. And, in fact, by* law, *I . . .* , implying that he is unable to talk due some kind of legal embargo, when really he is unable to talk about Lingk's acreage as there is nothing about it to impart.

Commentary

The modals and quasi-modals convey the irrealis. Deontic and epistemic modals are used to deliberately obfuscate. There is nothing real about Roma's lies.

4 Teaching Point

Like auxiliary *have, be* and *do*, the modal auxiliaries are small and frequent and can get overlooked by readers. However the fact they can carry both deontic and epistemic meanings can be useful for authors wanting to create ambiguity. Modal auxiliaries convey the irrealis, and both in fiction and real life, speakers spend much time speculating about nonfactual events.

12 On Aspect

1 Definition of term *aspect*

Tense refers to whether something happened in the past, is happening in the present, or will happen in the future. *Aspect* refers to whether that event is over or is on-going, regardless of when:

> *Julia ran a shop*
>
> *Julia had run a shop*
>
> *Julia was running a shop*
>
> *By 1934, Julia had been running her shop for ten years*

All of these refer to events in the past. The first example is a simple past tense verb, ran. The second, had run, implies that the event is now over, and is known as the *perfective* aspect. Perfectives correlate with *–ed* forms, and *run* is an *–ed* form here (Standard English changes the stem vowel to *ran* rather than adds *-ed* but linguists still call it the *-ed* form). The third, was running, implies that the event was on-going at the point of time under discussion, and is known as the *progressive* aspect. Progressives correlate with *–ing* forms. The fourth, a progressive usage, shows how auxiliaries can stack up: [aux *have* + aux *be* + *-ing*], in this case.

All this might sound quite complicated, but native speakers have no trouble at all with aspect. There is nothing especially sophisticated or linguistically adept about mixing tenses and the various auxiliaries + base forms, *–ed* and *–ing* forms, or stacking up auxiliary verbs.

2 Demonstration of term *aspect*

Read through the following text and identify the finite verbs, excluding modals.

Customers were pleased at first when l'Etrangère would provide them at a moment's notice with a suitcase, or a fox fur, or a pair of dress-preservers, or some gloves; but when the moment came, as it generally did, when there was some trouble over a fitting, or the delivery of a frock on time, then the shop people thought: 'And after all the trouble we have taken getting her a suitcase, dress-preservers, tooth-paste, and what-not, with no profit to ourselves . . . ' And the customer thought: 'After all, I daresay I could have got that suitcase, dress-preservers, tooth-paste, or what-not much better at a proper shop, and they can't be very real dressmakers or they wouldn't do such a thing, and if they only had been real dressmakers my frock would have fitted.' Meanwhile, Marian, Gipsy, and Julia would all be sitting up after hours frantically stitching, planning, and even eventually delivering the frock in a taxi so as to meet the requirements of a customer, who, quite unaware that a 'little' shop has no particular means of delivery, would remain as calm and unperturbed as though the gown had arrived in the natural course of events from Debenham & Freebody's.

F. Tennyson Jesse, 1934, *A Pin to See the Peepshow*

Fashion note: *dress-preservers*, otherwise known as *dress-shields*, were a vital piece of kit before the invention of deodorant: *Oxford English Dictionary* dress-shield *n.* 'a piece of waterproof or other material fastened under the arms of a woman's bodice to protect it from perspiration.'

Here is the extract again with finite Verb Phrases in blue, excluding modal constructions:

Customers were pleased at first when l'Etrangère would provide them at a moment's notice with a suitcase, or a fox fur, or a pair of dress-preservers, or some gloves; but when the moment came, as it generally did, when there was some trouble over a fitting, or the delivery of a frock on time, then the shop people thought: 'And after all the trouble we have taken getting her a suitcase, dress-preservers, tooth-paste, and what-not, with no profit to ourselves . . . ' And the customer thought: 'After all, I daresay I could have got that suitcase, dress-preservers, tooth-paste, or what-not much better at a proper shop, and they can't be very real dressmakers or they wouldn't do such a thing, and if they only had been real dressmakers my frock would have fitted.' Meanwhile, Marian, Gipsy, and Julia would all be sitting up after hours frantically stitching, planning, and even eventually delivering the frock in a taxi so as to meet the requirements of a customer, who, quite unaware that a 'little' shop has no particular means of delivery, would remain as calm and unperturbed as though the gown had arrived in the natural course of events from Debenham & Freebody's.

Here is a table indicating aspect:

Past tense	Non-past tense
Simple: came, did, was, thought, thought,	daresay, has
[aux *be* + *-ed*]: were pleased	
[aux *have* + *-ed*]: had been, had arrived	have taken

(continued)

Past tense	Non-past tense
[modal aux + aux *have* + *-ed*]: could have got, would have fitted	
[modal aux + aux *be* + *-ing*] would be sitting, stitching, planning, delivering	
[modal aux + base form]: would provide, wouldn't do, would remain	can't be

The table looks relatively complex, mixing past and non-past tenses and various progressive and perfective constructions – yet the passage was short and easy to understand. The point is that it is normal for authors to use all the machinery of aspect.

3 Literary Exercise

In the following text, the speaker is a detective. Identify the finite verbs and consider their aspect. Why do you think Chandler chose to use this aspect distribution?

The border people had nothing to say to us. Up on the windy mesa where the Tijuana Airport is I parked close to the office and just sat while Terry got his ticket. The propellers of the DC-3 were already turning over slowly, just enough to keep warm. A tall dreamboat of a pilot in a grey uniform was chatting with a group of four people. One was about six feet four and carried a gun case. There was a girl in slacks beside him, and a smallish middle-aged man and a grey-haired woman so tall that she made him look puny. Three or four obvious Mexicans were standing around as well. That seemed to be the load. The steps were at the door but nobody seemed anxious to get in. Then a Mexican flight steward came down the steps and stood waiting. There didn't seem to be any loudspeaker equipment. The Mexicans climbed into the plane but the pilot was still chatting with the Americans.

There was a big Packard parked next to me. I got out and took a gander at the license on the post. Maybe someday I'll learn to mind my own business. As I pulled my head out I saw the tall woman staring in my direction.

Then Terry came across the dusty gravel.

"I'm all set," he said. "This is where I say good-bye."

He put his hand out. I shook it. He looked pretty good now, just tired, just tired as all hell.

I lifted the pigskin suitcase out of the Olds and put it down on the gravel. He stared at it angrily.

"I told you I didn't want it," he said snappishly.

"There's a nice pint of hooch in it, Terry. Also some pyjamas and stuff. And it's all anonymous. If you don't want it, check it. Or throw it away."

"I have reasons," he said stiffly.

"So have I."

He smiled suddenly. He picked up the suitcase and squeezed my arm with his free hand. "Okay, pal. You're the boss. And remember, if things get tough, you have a blank check. You don't owe me a thing. We had a few drinks together and got to be friendly and I talked too much about me. I left five C notes in your coffee can. Don't be sore at me."

"I'd rather you hadn't."

"I'll never spend half of what I have."

"Good luck, Terry."

The two Americans were going up the steps into the plane. A squatty guy with a wide dark face came out of the door of the office building and waved and pointed.

"Climb aboard," I said. "I know you didn't kill her. That's why I'm here."

He braced himself. His whole body got stiff. He turned slowly, then looked back.

"I'm sorry," he said quietly. "But you're wrong about that. I'm going to walk quite slowly to the plane. You have plenty of time to stop me."

He walked. I watched him. The guy in the doorway of the office was waiting, but not too impatient. Mexicans seldom are. He reached down and patted the pigskin suitcase and grinned at Terry. Then he stood aside and Terry went through the door. In a little while Terry came out through the door on the other side, where the customs people are when you're coming in. He walked, still slowly, across the gravel to the steps. He stopped there and looked towards me. He didn't signal or wave. Neither did I. Then he went up into the plane, and the steps were pulled back.

I got into the Olds and started it and backed and turned and moved half-way across the parking space. The tall woman and the short man were still out on the field. The woman had a handkerchief out to wave. The plane began to taxi down to the end of the field, raising plenty of dust. It turned at the far end and the motors revved up in a thundering roar. It began to move forward picking up speed slowly.

The dust rose in clouds behind it. Then it was airborne. I watched it lift slowly into the gusty air and fade off into the naked blue sky to the south-east.

Then I left. Nobody at the border gate looked at me as if my face meant as much as the hands on a clock.

Raymond Chandler, 1954, *The Long Good-Bye*

Note on lexis: to *take a gander* is to take a look, *Oxford English Dictionary* gander, v. first attested in this context in 1887 in a book on Cheshire dialect in reference to the long swivelling neck of a peering goose. *Packard* and *Oldsmobile* were types of American car. *C notes* are hundred dollar bills.

Here is the text again marked with finite verbs in blue.

The border people had nothing to say to us. Up on the windy mesa where the Tijuana Airport is I parked close to the office and just sat while Terry got his ticket. The propellers of the DC-3 were already turning over slowly, just enough to keep warm. A tall dreamboat of a pilot in a grey uniform was chatting with a group of four people. One was about six feet four and carried a gun case. There was a girl in slacks beside him, and a smallish middle-aged man and a grey-haired woman so tall that she made him look puny. Three or four obvious Mexicans were standing around as well. That seemed to be the load. The steps were at the door but nobody seemed anxious to get in. Then a Mexican flight steward came down the steps and stood waiting. There didn't seem to be any loudspeaker equipment. The Mexicans climbed into the plane but the pilot was still chatting with the Americans.
    There was a big Packard parked next to me. I got out and took a gander at the license on the post. Maybe someday I'll learn to mind my own business. As I pulled my head out I saw the tall woman staring in my direction.
    Then Terry came across the dusty gravel.
    "I'm all set," he said. "This is where I say good-bye."
    He put his hand out. I shook it. He looked pretty good now, just tired, just tired as all hell.
    I lifted the pigskin suitcase out of the Olds and put it down on the gravel. He stared at it angrily.
    "I told you I didn't want it," he said snappishly.
    "There's a nice pint of hooch in it, Terry. Also some pyjamas and stuff. And it's all anonymous. If you don't want it, check it. Or throw it away."
    "I have reasons," he said stiffly.
    "So have I."
    He smiled suddenly. He picked up the suitcase and squeezed my arm with his free hand. "Okay, pal. You're the boss. And remember, if things get tough, you have a blank check. You don't owe me a thing. We had a few drinks together and got to be friendly and I talked too much about me. I left five C notes in your coffee can. Don't be sore at me."
    "I'd rather you hadn't."
    "I'll never spend half of what I have."
    "Good luck, Terry."
    The two Americans were going up the steps into the plane. A squatty guy with a wide dark face came out of the door of the office building and waved and pointed.
    "Climb aboard," I said. "I know you didn't kill her. That's why I'm here."
    He braced himself. His whole body got stiff. He turned slowly, then looked back.

"I'm sorry," he said quietly. "But you're wrong about that. I'm going to walk quite slowly to the plane. You have plenty of time to stop me."

He walked. I watched him. The guy in the doorway of the office was waiting, but not too impatient. Mexicans seldom are. He reached down and patted the pigskin suitcase and grinned at Terry. Then he stood aside and Terry went through the door. In a little while Terry came out through the door on the other side, where the customs people are when you're coming in. He walked, still slowly, across the gravel to the steps. He stopped there and looked towards me. He didn't signal or wave. Neither did I. Then he went up into the plane, and the steps were pulled back.

I got into the Olds and started it and backed and turned and moved half-way across the parking space. The tall woman and the short man were still out on the field. The woman had a handkerchief out to wave. The plane began to taxi down to the end of the field, raising plenty of dust. It turned at the far end and the motors revved up in a thundering roar. It began to move forward picking up speed slowly.

The dust rose in clouds behind it. Then it was airborne. I watched it lift slowly into the gusty air and fade off into the naked blue sky to the south-east.

Then I left. Nobody at the border gate looked at me as if my face meant as much as the hands on a clock.

Analysis

In *There was a big Packard parked next to me*, *parked* is a past participle *–ed* form (the words *which was* have been elided). There are many [*to* + base form]s, but they are not finite (a finite verb is marked for person, number and tense). In the sentence *If you don't want it, check it or throw it away* and in the sentence *Climb aboard*, the verbs *check*, *throw* and *climb* are imperatives. In the sentence *He didn't signal or wave* I have ignored *wave*, as the finite verb *didn't* is elided.

The aspect of the finite verbs is as follows:

Past tense	Non-past tense
Simple: had, parked, sat, got, was, carried, was, made, seemed, were, seemed, came, climbed, was, got, took, pulled, saw, came, put, shook, looked, lifted, put, stared, told, said, said, smiled, picked, squeezed, had, got, talked, left, came, waved, pointed, braced, got, turned, looked, said, walked, watched, reached, patted, grinned, stood, went, came, walked, stopped, looked, did, went, got, started, backed, turned, moved, were, had, began, turned, revved, began, rose, was, watched, fade, left, looked, meant	is, is, say, 's, 's, have, have, 're, get, have, have, know, 's, 'm, 'm, 're, have, are, are

(continued)

Past tense	Non-past tense
[aux *be* + *-ing*]: were turning, was chatting, were standing, was chatting, were going, was waiting, were pulled	'm going, 're coming
[aux *be* + *ed*]:	'm set
[main V + *-ing*]: stood waiting	
[aux *do* + base form]: didn't seem, didn't want, didn't kill, didn't signal	don't want, don't owe, Don't be
[modal aux + base form]:	'd, 'll learn,'ll spend
[aux *have* + *-ed*]: hadn't ('left the money' elided)	

There are a total of 115 finite verbs, of which 95 are simple verbs, and 20 are compound Verb Phrases expressing progressive and perfective aspect. (I've omitted *I'd rather you hadn't* from this count). This is a ratio of 83% simple to 17% compound. The range of different auxiliaries + base form, + *-ed* and + *–ing* is not particularly surprising, but the ratio is unusual. A more even spread is expected.

Commentary

The passage relates lots of small actions without an omniscient narrator telling us why. When the speaker leaves, he gets into his car, starts it, backs, turns, and moves off. You have to do all this to turn a car around to face the other way, but we are not simply told that he turned the car around, or just that he drove out of the airport, but that he backed, turned, and moved. Why so much precise detail?

The speaker is a detective, and what we are told are the things he observes. He doesn't know whether the individuals waiting on the airfield are going to turn out to be significant, and neither do we. We don't know what they are talking about, because he can't hear them. He doesn't know why the pilot lingers, or why the tall man carries a gun case, or if it matters, so neither do we. The simple aspect merely relates events, whereas perfectives and progressives allow us to make inferences about events completed and events on-going. Only in the passages of conversation is there a more even spread of perfectives, progressives and simple aspect.

The denouement comes with Terry's admission that he killed a female, but this is followed by another four paragraphs where all that happens is that Terry boards, the plane takes off and the speaker drives away. Chandler is expert in handling suspense – setting up passages of waiting, or nothing much happening, in an active way so that the reader is involved in figuring out the significance. He gives us time to ponder why the speaker allows Terry to leave. Is he inept? Or doesn't he believe him? We must read on to find out.

4 Teaching Point

Using the full range of aspect is quite usual; restricting aspect to one construction only is likely to sound marked in some way. In the case of Chandler's text, the simple aspect is used to limit the reader to the information available to the detective. It makes for a hallmark of style – indeed, one which other crime writers appreciated, and Chandler had reason to complain of plagiarism.

13 Adverbs

1 Definition of term *adverbs*

Adverbs modify verbs, and other adverbs, and adjectives, although not all adverbs can do all three jobs. Prototypical adverbs are formed by adding *–ly* to an adjective: *silently, loudly, mostly, disastrously, fortunately, merrily, hopelessly, fantastically*:

She sings happily	(modifying the verb *sings*)
She sings quite happily	(the adverb *quite* is modifying the adverb *happily*)
She is truly happy	(the adverb *truly* is modifying the adjective *happy*)
Indeed she really is honestly, thoroughly happy	(the adverb really modifies the verb *is*, and adverbs honestly and thoroughly modify the adjective *happy*. Indeed is a sentence adverb, modifying the whole sentence.)

In older texts and regional dialect, adverbs do not always take *–ly* where we might expect:

go careful   exceeding good   I did it quite easy

Adverbs can be gradable:

despicably   very despicably
rapidly   extremely rapidly
Run quick! quickly, very quickly, absolutely directly!

Very and *extremely* are themselves adverbs, known as Degree Adverbs because they specify the degree to which an adjective or another adverb applies. Degree adverbs include *too, entirely, highly, quite, totally, almost, barely*. Degree adverbs are not gradable (**too quite, *very almost*).

Adverbs can take comparative and superlative forms:

happily   more happily   most happily

Some high-frequency adverbs are irregular:

much (more, most) [compare *Ta muchly*]
well (better, best)

badly (worse, worst)
little (less, least)

Further, there are adverbs of place, manner and time:

now, then   (adverbs of time)
there, here (adverbs of place)
slowly, well (adverbs of manner)

2 Demonstration of term *adverbs*

Read these verses about the Great Fire of London in 1666. John Dryden wrote them soon after:

> Such was the rise of this prodigious fire,
>   Which in mean buildings first obscurely bred,
> From thence did soon to open streets aspire,
>   And straight to Palaces and Temples spread.
>
> The diligence of Trades and noiseful gain,
>   And luxury, more late, asleep were laid:
> All was the nights, and in her silent reign,
>   No sound the rest of Nature did invade.
>
> In this deep quiet, from what scource unknown,
>   Those seeds of fire their fatal birth disclose:
> And first, few scatt'ring sparks about were blown,
>   Big with the flames that to our ruine rose.
>
> Then, in some close-pent room it crept along,
>   And, smouldring as it went, in silence fed:
> Till th'infant monster, with devouring strong,
>   Walk'd boldly upright with exalted head.
>
> Now, like some rich or mighty Murderer,
>   To great for prison, which he breaks with gold:
> Who fresher for new mischiefs does appear,
>   And dares the world to tax him with the old.
>
> So scapes th'insulting fire his narrow Jail,
>   And makes small out-lets into open air:
> There the fierce winds his open force assail,
>   And beat him down-ward to his first repair.

The winds, like crafty Courtezans, with-held
　　His flames from burning, but to blow them more:
And, every fresh attempt, he is repell'd
　　With faint denials, weaker than before.

And now, no longer letted of his prey,
　　He leaps up at it with inrag'd desire:
O'r-looks the neighbours with a wide survey,
　　And nods at every house his threatning fire.

John Dryden, 1667, *Annus Mirabilis: The Year of Wonders*, verses 215–222

Transcribed from Early English Books Online

Here is the extract from the poem again, with the adverbs in blue.

215
Such was the rise of this prodigious fire,
　　Which in mean buildings first obscurely bred,
From thence did soon to open streets aspire,
　　And straight to Palaces and Temples spread.
216
The diligence of Trades and noiseful gain,
　　And luxury, more late, asleep were laid:
All was the nights, and in her silent reign,
　　No sound the rest of Nature did invade.
217
In this deep quiet, from what scource unknown,
　　Those seeds of fire their fatal birth disclose:
And first, few scatt'ring sparks about were blown,
　　Big with the flames that to our ruine rose.
218
Then, in some close-pent room it crept along,
　　And, smouldring as it went, in silence fed:
Till th'infant monster, with devouring strong,
　　Walk'd boldly upright with exalted head.
219
Now, like some rich or mighty Murderer,
　　To great for prison, which he breaks with gold:
Who fresher for new mischiefs does appear,
　　And dares the world to tax him with the old.
220
So scapes th'insulting fire his narrow Jail,
　　And makes small out-lets into open air:
There the fierce winds his open force assail,
　　And beat him down-ward to his first repair.

221
The winds, like crafty Courtezans, with-held
    His flames from burning, but to blow them more:
And, every fresh attempt, he is repell'd
    With faint denials, weaker than before.
222
And now, no longer letted of his prey,
    He leaps up at it with inrag'd desire:
O'r-looks the neighbours with a wide survey,
    And nods at every house his threatning fire.

Adverbs of time: *first, soon, more late, first, then, now, before, now, no longer*

Adverbs of place: *thence, there*

Adverbs of manner: *obscurely, straight, boldly, upright, fresher*

In verse 215, *obscurely* modifies the verb *bred*, *soon* modifies the Verb Phrase *did aspire*, and *straight* modifies *spread*. This is a little microcosm of the fire, bred in obscurity, soon taking hold, and spreading straight.

In verse 221, *but* is used as an adverb with the sense of 'only' ('the winds withheld his flames only to blow them more').

Verse 216 is not about the fire but about the silence of the night. It is not an easy verse to understand, so let's reorder the components and repunctuate:

> The diligence of trades and noiseful gain and luxury were more late laid asleep:
> All was the night's, and in her silent reign, the rest of Nature did invade no sound.

To paraphrase: the noise of trade and commerce and luxury were lately laid to sleep; everything belonged to the night, and in her silent reign, the rest of Nature made no sound. There are two ambiguities: *more late*, and *rest*. To take the second first, is it the repose of Nature or the remainder of Nature? Whichever you choose, the soundlessness of Nature is the main semantic point: the night was silent. Were the noises of the day laid to sleep *more late*, 'later on in the evening', or, 'more recently, lately'? I have chosen the second meaning in my paraphrase, but both senses were operative in 1667 (*Oxford English Dictionary* late, adv. 3. 'at or until a time far into the day or night'; 5. a. 'recently, of late, in recent times', both attested before the 1200s).

In verses 218 and 219 the adverbs help to personify the fire as an infant monster walking boldly and a murderer reappearing more fresh for new mischiefs, with *boldly upright* modifying the verb *walk* and *fresher* modifying the Verb Phrase *does appear*. (Alternatively, you could analyse *upright* as an adjective modifying *monster*.) In verse 222, having escaped from his prison, the personified fire is no longer letted of his prey (meaning 'baulked'; *Oxford English Dictionary* let, *v.²*. *a* 'to hinder, prevent, obstruct, stand in the way of') as he spies more houses to burn. *No longer* modifies *letted*.

Adverbs, then, do many jobs and sit in many places in the sentence, both in the Verb Phrase and the Noun Phrase. In these verses, the adverbs of place and time are function words [function words have less semantic content and more grammatical function in a text], whereas it is the adverbs of manner that are lexical items. Dryden is more interested in conveying how the flames spread, than when or where.

3 Literary Exercise

Here is another poem about rapid movement in London, depicting the morning rush-hour in 1800. Spot the adverbs. How do they compare with the adjectives – which type of modifier is doing the most work?

London Summer's Morning

Who has not wak'd to list the busy sounds
Of Summer's Morning, in the sultry smoke
Of noisy London? On the pavement hot
The sooty chimney-boy, with dingy face
And tatter'd covering, shrilly bawls his trade,
Rousing the sleepy housemaid. At the door
The milk-pail rattles, and the tinkling bell
Proclaims the dustman's office, while the street
Is lost in clouds impervious. Now begins
The din of hackney coaches, waggons, carts;
While tinmans' shops, and noisy trunk-makers,
Knife-grinders, coopers, squeaking cork-cutters,
Fruit-barrows, and the hunger-giving cries
Of vegetable venders, fill the air.
Now ev'ry shop displays its varied trade,
And the fresh-sprinkled pavement cools the feet
Of early walkers. At the private door
The ruddy housemaid twirls the busy mop,
Annoying the smart 'prentice, or neat girl,
Tripping with band-box lightly. Now the sun
Darts burning splendour on the glitt'ring pane,
Save where the canvas awning throws a shade
On the gay merchandize. Now, spruce and trim,
In shops (where Beauty smiles with Industry,)
Sits the smart damsel, while the passenger

>   Peeps thro' the window, watching ev'ry charm.
>   Now pastry dainties catch the eyes minute
>   Of humming insects, while the limy snare
>   Waits to enthral them. Now the lamp-lighter
>   Mounts the tall ladder, nimbly vent'rous,
>   To trim the half fill'd lamp; while at his feet
>   The pot-boy yells discordant ! all along
>   The sultry pavement, the old-cloathsman cries
>   In tone monotonous, and side-long views
>   The area, for his traffic. Now the bag
>   Is slily open'd, and the half-worn suit
>   (Sometimes the pilfer'd treasure of the base
>   Domestic spoiler), for one half its worth,
>   Sinks in the green abyss. The porter now
>   Bears his huge load along the burning way,
>   And the poor Poet wakes from busy dreams,
>   To paint the Summer Morning.

Mary Robinson, 1800, *London's Summer Morning*
Transcribed from the *Whitehall Evening Post*, August 21–21 1800, Issue 8281

Note on lexis: *Oxford English Dictionary* bandbox, *n.* a. A slight box of card-board or very thin chip covered with paper, for collars, caps, hats, and millinery; originally made for the 'bands' or ruffs of the 17th cent.

Oxford English Dictionary area, *n.* I. 2. b. A sunken court giving access to the basement of a house, separated from the pavement by railings, with a flight of steps providing access.

Oxford English Dictionary spoiler, *n.* 1. a. One who pillages, plunders, or robs.

The base domestic spoiler is a burglar; the area into which the old-clothesman peers sidelong, looking for a servant to emerge, is the basement well between the railings and the house frontage. The green abyss is likely to be this area, green with plants, where the transaction takes place.

Here is the poem again with the adverbs in blue.

>   WHO has not wak'd to list the busy sounds
>   Of Summer's Morning, in the sultry smoke
>   Of noisy London? On the pavement hot
>   The sooty chimney-boy, with dingy face
>   And tatter'd covering, shrilly bawls his trade,
>   Rousing the sleepy housemaid. At the door
>   The milk-pail rattles, and the tinkling bell
>   Proclaims the dustman's office, while the street

Is lost in clouds impervious. Now begins
The din of hackney coaches, waggons, carts;
While tinmans' shops, and noisy trunk-makers,
Knife-grinders, coopers, squeaking cork-cutters,
Fruit-barrows, and the hunger-giving cries
Of vegetable venders, fill the air.
Now ev'ry shop displays its varied trade,
And the fresh-sprinkled pavement cools the feet
Of early walkers. At the private door
The ruddy housemaid twirls the busy mop,
Annoying the smart 'prentice, or neat girl,
Tripping with band-box lightly. Now the sun
Darts burning splendour on the glitt'ring pane,
Save where the canvas awning throws a shade
On the gay merchandize. Now, spruce and trim,
In shops (where Beauty smiles with Industry,)
Sits the smart damsel, while the passenger
Peeps thro' the window, watching ev'ry charm.
Now pastry dainties catch the eyes minute
Of humming insects, while the limy snare
Waits to enthral them. Now the lamp-lighter
Mounts the tall ladder, nimbly vent'rous,
To trim the half fill'd lamp; while at his feet
The pot-boy yells discordant ! all along
The sultry pavement, the old-cloathsman cries
In tone monotonous, and side-long views
The area, for his traffic. Now the bag
Is slily open'd, and the half-worn suit
(Sometimes the pilfer'd treasure of the base
Domestic spoiler), for one half its worth,
Sinks in the green abyss. The porter now
Bears his huge load along the burning way,
And the poor Poet wakes from busy dreams,
To paint the Summer Morning.

Analysis

Adjectives predominate by 54:20 –

Adjectives and their Nouns	Adverbs and their Verbs
busy sounds	shrilly bawls
Summer's Morning	now
sultry smoke	now

(continued)

Adjectives and their Nouns	Adverbs and their Verbs
noisy London	tripping lightly
pavement hot	now
sooty chimney-boy	where
dingy face	Now
tatter'd covering	spruce sits
sleepy housemaid	trim sits
tinkling bell	where
dustman's office	Now
clouds impervious	now
hackney coaches	nimbly
tinmans' shops	yells discordant
noisy trunk-makers	all
Knife-grinders	side-long views
squeaking cork-cutters	now
Fruit-barrows	slily open'd
hunger-giving cries	sometimes
vegetable venders	now
varied trade	
fresh-sprinkled pavement	
early walkers	
private door	
ruddy housemaid	
busy mop	
smart 'prentice	
neat girl	
band-box	
burning splendour	
glitt'ring pane	
canvas awning	
gay merchandize	
smart damsel	
pastry dainties	
eyes minute	
humming insects	
limy snare	
lamp-lighter	
tall ladder	
half fill'd lamp	
pot-boy	
sultry pavement	
old-cloathsman	
tone monotonous	
half-worn suit	

(continued)

Adjectives and their Nouns	Adverbs and their Verbs
pilfer'd treasure	
base Domestic spoiler	
green abyss	
huge load	
burning way	
poor Poet	
busy dreams	
Summer Morning	

Adverbs of time: *now, now, now, now, now, now, now, now, sometimes*

Adverbs of place: *where, where*

Adverbs of manner: *shrilly, lightly, spruce, trim, nimbly, discordant, side-long, slily*

Word-order is not always as expected. This is known as *inversion*:

> *side-long views* rather than *views side-long*
> *eyes minute* rather than *minute eyes*
> *clouds impervious* rather than *impervious clouds*
> *tone monotonous* rather than *monotonous tone*
> *pavement hot* rather than *hot pavement*

Inversion is typical of poetry of the period, and some critics found it annoying.

Notice how adverbs in *–ly* had not yet settled down to one immutable form: compare *yells discordant* with *come quick, go slow, look sharp*.

Commentary

Although the poem is full of noisy movement, this is largely conveyed via the Noun Phrase, either [adjective + noun] or [noun + adjective]. But the poem is about the moment of waking and hearing all the hubbub, and whilst the adverbs of manner are relatively striking (especially when inverted or lacking an expected *–ly*), the eight tokens of *now*, easily overlooked, point to the last couplet where the poet wakes to write her poem.

4 Teaching Point

Adverbs can modify verbs, adjectives and other adverbs. You might expect topics dealing with movement (like the rapid spread of fire or the rush-hour) to take many verbs and adverbs, but (and this is a generalization against which individual texts may fail) literary texts usually contain many more adjectives modifying nouns than they do adverbs modifying verbs, regardless of subject. The smaller adverbs (*now, there, here*) tend to preponderate and, like prepositions, serve to anchor a text in time and space.

14 Adverbials

1 Definition of term *adverbials*

Adverbs, Adverb Phrases and Prepositional Phrases can function as a unit known as an *adverbial* – as can some nouns, Noun Phrases and subordinate clauses. Adverbials modify the verb. They can usually be moved or deleted without leaving the sentence ungrammatical or nonsense, and often answer questions such as why? when? how? where?

> Yesterday I went to a meeting at the University of Bristol.
>
> [At the University of Bristol] [yesterday] I went to a meeting
>
> [0] I went to a meeting [0].

[At the University of Bristol] and [yesterday] tell us something about where and when I went, and are movable and deletable, and so they qualify as adverbials.

2 Demonstration of adverbials

In this chapter there are two demonstrations, the first performed on a relatively direct and straightforward kind of text, and the second on more experimental writing. Here's the first one:

He had first met his wife during carnival in a seaside town in Jacmel. His favorite part of the festivities was the finale, on the day before Ash Wednesday, when a crowd of tired revelers would gather on the beach to burn their carnival masks and costumes and feign weeping, symbolically purging themselves of the carousing of the preceding days and nights. She had volunteered to be one of the official weepers, one of those who wailed most convincingly as the carnival relics turned to ashes in the bonfire.
    "Papa Kanaval ou ale! Farewell Father Carnival!" she howled, with real tears running down her face.
    If she could grieve so passionately on demand, he thought, perhaps she could love even more. After the other weepers had left, she stayed behind until the last embers of the carnival bonfire had dimmed. It was impossible to distract her, to make her laugh. She could never fake weeping, she told him. Every time she cried for anything, she cried for everything else that had ever hurt her.

He had traveled between Jacmel and Port-au-Prince while he was waiting for his visa to come through. And when he finally had a travel date he asked her to marry him.

One New York afternoon, when he came home from work, he found her sitting on the edge of the bed in that small room, staring at the pictures of herself on the opposite wall. She didn't move as he kissed the top of her head. He said nothing, simply slipped out of his clothes and lay down on the bed, pressing his face against her back. He did not want to trespass on her secrets. He simply wanted to extinguish the carnivals burning in her head.

Edwidge Danticat, 2002, *Seven*

Here's the text again, with the adverbials in green:

He had [first] met his wife [during carnival] [in a seaside town] [in Jacmel]. His favorite part of the festivities was the finale, [on the day before Ash Wednesday], [when a crowd of tired revelers would gather] [on the beach] [to burn their carnival masks and costumes and feign weeping], [symbolically] [purging themselves of the carousing] [of the preceding days and nights]. She had volunteered to be one of the official weepers, one of those who wailed [most convincingly] [as the carnival relics turned to ashes] [in the bonfire].

"Papa Kanaval ou ale! Farewell Father Carnival!" she howled, [with real tears running] [down her face].

[If she could grieve] [so passionately] [on demand], he thought, perhaps she could love [even more]. [After the other weepers had left], she stayed behind [until the last embers of the carnival bonfire had dimmed]. It was impossible to distract her, to make her laugh. She could [never] fake weeping, she told him. [Every time] she cried [for anything], she cried [for everything else that had ever hurt her].

He had traveled [between Jacmel and Port-au-Prince] [while he was waiting] [for his visa to come through]. And [when he [finally] had a travel date] he asked her to marry him.

[One New York afternoon], [when he came home from work], he found her [sitting [on the edge of the bed] [in that small room]], [staring [at the pictures of herself] [on the opposite wall]]. She didn't move [as he kissed the top of her head]. He said nothing, [simply] slipped [out of his clothes] and lay down [on the bed], [pressing his face [against her back]]. He did not want to trespass [on her secrets]. He [simply] wanted to extinguish the carnivals burning [in her head].

To find the adverbials, I first identified the verb and then tried moving the elements I suspected of modifying it, e.g.:

> He had first met his wife: he had met his wife first
>
> He had first met his wife during carnival: during carnival he had first met his wife
>
> He had first met his wife during carnival in a seaside town: he had met his wife first in a seaside town during carnival
>
> He had first met his wife during carnival in a seaside town in Jacmel: during carnival in Jacmel he had met his wife first in a seaside town

This kind of switching elements around allows you to see how the author foregrounded the meeting (coming at the beginning of the sentence) and the setting, Jacmel (coming at the end). The adverbial forms in this sentence are Prepositional Phrases and an adverb (*first*), and the function is to give information about the verb *met* – the when and the where this meeting took place.

Often, adverbials are embedded in larger units:

> One New York afternoon, when he came home [from work], he found her [sitting [on the edge of the bed] [in that small room]], [staring [at the pictures of herself] [on the opposite wall]].

To confirm that we've identified the adverbials correctly, try rearranging them, as, e.g.:

> on the edge of the bed, in that small room, staring at the pictures of herself on the opposite wall, sitting, he found her

The second sentence in the extract can be interpreted in two ways:

> His favorite part of the festivities was the finale, on the day before Ash Wednesday, when a crowd of tired revelers would gather on the beach to burn their carnival masks and costumes and feign weeping, symbolically purging themselves of the carousing of the preceding days and nights.

either:

> when a crowd of tired revelers would gather . . . and feign weeping

or:

> when a crowd of tired revelers would gather [to burn their masks . . . and feign weeping]

In the first interpretation, the base forms *gather* and *feign* are both governed by the modal auxiliary *would*. In the second interpretation, *feign* is a base form governed by the preposition *to*. The form of the highlighted unit in this second interpretation is two non-finite clauses, [*to burn their masks*] and [*to feign weeping*], with the second *to* elided. Both clauses modify the Verb Phrase *would gather*, expressing purposive meaning.

Is there a difference in meaning? The second interpretation with the adverbial is rather more purposeful; in the first, gathering is just something the revellers do by tradition. Does it matter much? This depends on your literary judgement. Ambiguities in interpretation are always going to be of interest to a literature student, but in my judgement, not a lot hangs on it here as the main focus of the paragraph is not the revelers – but you may disagree with me. I may have missed a nuance.

Let's split the adverbials up into *how, where, when, why*:

How: symbolically, purging themselves of the carousing of the preceding days and nights, most convincingly, with real tears running down her face, so passionately, on demand, even more, staring at the pictures of herself, simply, out of his clothes, pressing his face, simply

Where: in a seaside town, in Jacmel, on the beach, between Jacmel and Port-au-Prince, sitting on the edge of the bed in that small room, on the opposite wall, on the bed, against her back, on her secrets, in her head

When: first, during carnival, on the day before Ash Wednesday, when a crowd of tired revelers would gather, as the carnival relics turned to ashes in the bonfire, after the other weepers had left, until the last embers of the carnival bonfire had dimmed, never, every time, while he was waiting for his visa to come through, when he finally had a travel date, one New York afternoon, when he came home from work, as he kissed the top of her head

Why: to burn their carnival masks and costumes and feign weeping, for anything, for everything else that had ever hurt her

Grouping the adverbials like this reveals that time-frames are detailed whereas causative reasons are not. The anything and everything that has caused the wife's pain is not described, but the different time-frames convey the duration and intensity of her grief.

Here is the second demonstration of adverbial analysis, this time an analysis of a Modernist text. Modernism was an experimental movement, and several of its practitioners experimented with language. In this case, it makes adverbial analysis fiendish as there is a lot of modification – remember, adverbials modify the Verb Phrase, not the Noun Phrase. This text is a challenge for analysers of adverbials!

At the same great hotel in which they held their Sunday luncheons Mrs Weatherby reserved a private room to entertain old friends in honour of Philip's twenty firster.

Standing prepared, empty, curtained, shuttered, tall mirrors facing across laid tables crowned by napkins, with space rocketing transparence from one glass silvered surface to the other, supporting walls covered in olive coloured silk, chandeliers repeated to a thousand thousand profiles to be lost in olive gray depths as quiet as this room's untenanted attention, but a scene made warm with mass upon mass of daffodils banked up against mirrors, or mounded once on each of the round white tables and laid in a flat frieze about their edges, – here then time stood still for Jane, even in wine bottles over to one side holding the single movement, and that unseen of bubbles rising just as the air, similarly trapped even if conditioned, watched unseen across itself in a superb but not indifferent pause of mirrors.

Into this waiting shivered one small seen movement that seemed to snap the room apart, a door handle turning.

Then with a cry unheard, sung now, unuttered then by hinges and which fled back to creation in those limitless centuries of staring glass, with a shriek only of silent motion the portals came ajar with as it were an unoperated clash of cymbal to usher Mrs Weatherby in, her fine head made tiny by the intrusion perhaps because she was alone, but upon which, as upon a rising swell of violas untouched by bows strung from none other than the manes of unicorns that quiet wait was ended, the room could gather itself up at last.

Henry Green, 1950, *Nothing*

Here's the text again, with the adverbials marked in green.

[At the same great hotel in which they held their Sunday luncheons] **Mrs Weatherby reserved a private room** [to entertain old friends] [in honour of Philip's twenty firster].

[Standing prepared, empty, curtained, shuttered], [tall mirrors facing across laid tables crowned by napkins], [with space rocketing transparence from one glass silvered surface to the other], [supporting walls covered in olive coloured silk], **chandeliers repeated** [to a thousand thousand profiles to be lost in olive gray depths as quiet as this room's untenanted attention], **but a scene made warm** [with mass upon mass of daffodils banked up against mirrors, or mounded once on each of the round white tables and laid in a flat frieze about their edges], – [here] [then] **time stood still** [for Jane], [even in wine bottles over to one side holding the single movement, and that unseen of bubbles rising just as the air, similarly trapped even if conditioned], [watched unseen across itself in a superb but not indifferent pause of mirrors].

[Into this waiting] **shivered one small seen movement that seemed to snap the room apart, a door handle turning.**

[Then] [with a cry unheard], **sung** [now], **unuttered** [then] [by hinges and which fled back to creation] [in those limitless centuries of staring glass], [with a shriek only of silent motion] **the portals came ajar** [with as it were an unoperated clash of cymbal] [to usher Mrs Weatherby in], [her fine head made tiny] [by the intrusion] [perhaps because she was alone], **but upon which,** [as upon a rising swell of violas untouched by bows strung from none other than the manes of unicorns that quiet wait was ended], **the room could gather itself up** [at last].

Below I have divided the sentences up into macro-adverbials (that is, larger rather than smaller movable units) and moved them around. There are many places to move them; as the first sentence is short I've presented two options:

Sentence One: *Henry Green's original*
At the same great hotel in which they held their Sunday luncheons Mrs Weatherby reserved a private room to entertain old friends in honour of Philip's twenty firster.

Repositioned adverbials:
a) **Mrs Weatherby reserved a private room** [at the same great hotel in which they held their Sunday luncheons] [to entertain old friends] [in honour of Philip's twenty firster]
b) [In honour of Philip's twenty firster] **Mrs Weatherby reserved a private room** [at the same great hotel in which they held their Sunday luncheons] [to entertain old friends]

In a) and b), Mrs Weatherby and the party come first, whereas in the original, it is the hotel which is foregrounded. Although Philip's mother's party is the reason for the description, the hotel is really the protagonist of the passage.

Sentence Two: *Henry Green's original*
Standing prepared, empty, curtained, shuttered, tall mirrors facing across laid tables crowned by napkins, with space rocketing transparence from one glass silvered surface to the other, supporting walls covered in olive coloured silk, chandeliers repeated to a thousand thousand profiles to be lost in olive gray depths as quiet as this room's untenanted attention, but a scene made warm with mass upon mass of daffodils banked up against mirrors, or mounded once on each of the round white tables and laid in a flat frieze about their edges, – here then time stood still for Jane, even in wine bottles over to one side holding the single movement, and

that unseen of bubbles rising just as the air, similarly trapped even if conditioned, watched unseen across itself in a superb but not indifferent pause of mirrors.

Repositioned adverbials:
[With space rocketing transparence from one glass silvered surface to the other], [supporting walls covered in olive coloured silk], [to a thousand thousand profiles to be lost in olive gray depths as quiet as this room's untenanted attention], **chandeliers repeated** [tall mirrors facing across laid tables crowned by napkins], [with mass upon mass of daffodils banked up against mirrors, or mounded once on each of the round white tables and laid in a flat frieze about their edges], [standing prepared, empty, curtained, shuttered], **but a scene made warm** – [even in wine bottles over to one side holding the single movement, and that unseen of bubbles rising just as the air, similarly trapped even if conditioned], [watched unseen across itself in a superb but not indifferent pause of mirrors], [here] [then] [for Jane], **time stood still.**

There are many other possibilities of adverbial placement, and this is not an easy sentence to process, but repositioning the adverbials shows that the undeletable, unmovable matter concerns the repetition of the chandeliers in the mirrors, the warmth of the scene, and how time stood still.

Sentence Three: *Henry Green's original*
Into this waiting shivered one small seen movement that seemed to snap the room apart, a door handle turning.

Repositioned adverbials:
One small seen movement that seemed to snap the room apart, a door handle turning, shivered [into this waiting].

The *one small seen movement* and the *door handle turning* are simultaneously the subject of the verb *shivered*, as they are one and the same thing. [that seemed to snap the room apart] postmodifies the noun *movement*. The repositioning of the adverbial shows that the original ordering foregrounded the waiting rather than the movement of the door.

Sentence Four: *Henry Green's original*
Then with a cry unheard, sung now, unuttered then by hinges and which fled back to creation in those limitless centuries of staring glass, with a shriek only of silent motion the portals came ajar with as it were an unoperated clash of cymbal to usher Mrs Weatherby in, her fine head made tiny by the intrusion perhaps because she was alone, but upon which, as upon a rising swell of violas untouched by bows strung from none other than the manes of unicorns that quiet wait was ended, the room could gather itself up at last.

Repositioned adverbials:
[To usher Mrs Weatherby in], [perhaps because she was alone] [her fine head made tiny by the intrusion], [with as it were an unoperated clash of cymbal, the portals [then] came ajar [in those limitless centuries of staring glass] [with a cry unheard], sung [now], unuttered [then] [by hinges and which fled back to creation], [with a shriek only of silent motion], but upon which, [as upon a rising swell of violas untouched by bows strung from none other than the manes of unicorns that quiet wait was ended], [at last], the room could gather itself up.

Again, there are many possibilities, this is just one manipulation. Whichever way the adverbials are repositioned, and despite Mrs Weatherby's presence in the fourth sentence, deleting or backgrounding the adverbials shows that it is the portals and the gathering unto itself of the room that are of significance here, not the humans.

Let's look at how they break down into how, why, when and where:

How: [Standing prepared, empty, curtained, shuttered], [tall mirrors facing across laid tables crowned by napkins], [with space rocketing transparence from one glass silvered surface to the other], [supporting walls covered in olive coloured silk], [to a thousand thousand profiles to be lost in olive gray depths as quiet as this room's untenanted attention], [with mass upon mass of daffodils banked up against mirrors, or mounded once on each of the round white tables and laid in a flat frieze about their edges], [watched unseen across itself in a superb but not indifferent pause of mirrors], [with a cry unheard], [by hinges which fled back to creation], [with a shriek only of silent motion], [with as it were an unoperated clash of cymbal], [her fine head made tiny], [by the intrusion], [as upon a rising swell of violas untouched by bows strung from none other than the manes of unicorns that quiet wait was ended]

Where: [At the same great hotel in which they held their Sunday luncheons], [here], [even in wine bottles over to one side holding the single movement, and that unseen of bubbles rising just as the air, similarly trapped even if conditioned], [into this waiting], [in those limitless centuries of staring glass]

Why: [to entertain old friends], [in honour of Philip's twenty firster.], [for Jane], [to usher Mrs Weatherby in], [perhaps because she was alone]

When: [then], [then], [now], [then], [at last]

Adverbials of manner dominate, the adverbials which answer the question *how* – standing, facing, rocketing, supporting, banked up, mounded, watched, with a shriek, by hinges, with an unoperated clash of cymbal, upon a rising swell of violas.

These adverbials largely contain -*ing* and –*ed* forms of verbs to do with sound and movement. There is an incongruity between the parts of speech and the thing described, a mirrored room. The room and its decorations are inanimate, but they are animated by a prescience of events about to happen.

Chandeliers repeating in mirrors in the Ritz Hotel, London https://www.theritzlondon.com.

3 Literary Exercise

Here is the beginning of Chapter Three from F. Scott Fitzgerald's *The Great Gatsby*, which also describes a party venue. What work are the adverbials doing in this text?

There was music from my neighbour's house through the summer nights. In his blue gardens men and girls came and went like moths among the whisperings and the champagne and the stars. At high tide in the afternoon I watched his guests diving from the tower of his raft, or taking the sun on the hot sand of his beach while his two motor-boats slit the waters of the Sound, drawing aquaplanes over cataracts of foam. On week-ends his Rolls-Royce became an omnibus, bearing parties to and from the city between nine in the morning and long past midnight, while his station wagon scampered like a brisk yellow bug to meet all trains. And on Mondays eight servants, including an extra gardener, toiled all day with mops and scrubbing-brushes and hammers and garden-shears, repairing the ravages of the night before.
    Every Friday five crates of oranges and lemons arrived from a fruiterer in New York – every Monday these same oranges and lemons left his back door in a pyramid of pulpless halves. There was a machine in the kitchen which could extract the juice of two hundred oranges in half an hour if a little button was pressed two hundred times by a butler's thumb.

At least once a fortnight a corps of caterers came down with several hundred feet of canvas and enough coloured lights to make a Christmas tree of Gatsby's enormous garden. On buffet tables, garnished with glistening hors-d'oeuvre, spiced baked hams crowded against salads of harlequin designs and pastry pigs and turkeys bewitched to a dark gold. In the main hall a bar with a real brass rail was set up, and stocked with gins and liquors and with cordials so long forgotten that most of his female guests were to young to know one from another.

F. Scott Fitzgerald, 1926, *The Great Gatsby*

Here is the text again, with the adverbials in green.

There was music [from my neighbour's house] [through the summer nights]. [In his blue gardens] **men and girls came and went** [like moths] [among the whisperings and the champagne and the stars]. [At high tide in the afternoon] **I watched his guests** [diving from the tower of his raft], [or taking the sun on the hot sand of his beach] [while his two motor-boats slit the waters of the Sound], [drawing aquaplanes over cataracts of foam]. [On week-ends] **his Rolls-Royce became an omnibus**, [bearing parties to and from the city] [between nine in the morning and long past midnight], [while his station wagon scampered [like a brisk yellow bug] [to meet all trains]]. [And on Mondays] **eight servants**, [including an extra gardener], **toiled** [all day] [with mops and scrubbing-brushes and hammers and garden-shears], [repairing the ravages of the night before].

[Every Friday] **five crates of oranges and lemons arrived** [from a fruiterer in New York] – [every Monday] **these same oranges and lemons left his back door** [in a pyramid of pulpless halves]. **There was a machine** [in the kitchen] **which could extract the juice of two hundred oranges** [in half an hour] [if a little button was pressed [two hundred times] [by a butler's thumb]].

[At least once a fortnight] **a corps of caterers came down** [with several hundred feet of canvas and enough coloured lights to make a Christmas tree of Gatsby's enormous garden]. [On buffet tables, garnished with glistening hors-d'oeuvre], **spiced baked hams crowded** [against salads of harlequin designs and pastry pigs and turkeys bewitched to a dark gold]. [In the main hall] **a bar** [with a real brass rail] **was set up, and stocked** [with gins and liquors and with cordials so long forgotten that most of his female guests were to young to know one from another].

Analysis

Splitting up the adverbials into how, why, when and where:

How: [like moths], [diving from the tower of his raft], [or taking the sun on the hot sand of his beach], [drawing aquaplanes over cataracts of foam], [bearing parties to and from the city], [including an extra gardener], [with mops and scrubbing-brushes and hammers and garden-shears], [in a pyramid of pulpless halves], [if a little button was pressed [two hundred times] [by a butler's thumb]], [with several hundred feet of canvas and enough coloured lights to make a Christmas tree of Gatsby's enormous garden], [garnished with glistening hors-d'oeuvre], [against salads of harlequin designs and pastry pigs and turkeys bewitched to a dark gold], [with a real brass rail], [with gins and liquors and with cordials so long forgotten that most of his female guests were to young to know one from another]

When: [through the summer nights], [at high tide in the afternoon], [while his two motor-boats slit the waters of the Sound], [On week-ends], [between nine in the morning and long past midnight], [while his station wagon scampered [like a brisk yellow bug] [to meet all trains]], [And on Mondays], [all day], [Every Friday], [every Monday], [in half an hour], [At least once a fortnight]

Where: [from my neighbour's house], [In his blue gardens], [among the whisperings and the champagne and the stars], [from a fruiterer in New York], [in the kitchen], [On buffet tables], [In the main hall]

Why: [repairing the ravages of the night before]

Commentary

Here, the rooms and their contents do not figure, and although the men, girls and guests are mentioned in the unmovable and undeletable content, the main focus of the undeletable subjects is the service personnel and their machines: the Rolls-Royce, the eight servants, the catering corps and their tools, the food and drink. (Notice how adverbial-analysis leads straight to the essential core of a text.) Splitting the adverbials into their functional purpose reveals that the passage is mainly concerned with *how*, the mechanism and logistics of how the parties functioned. In F. Scott Fitzgerald's text, Gatsby's parties, although sounding glamorous and pleasurable, are shown to be a lot of work for a lot of people.

4 Teaching Point

You will recall that premodification in the Noun Phrase is optional (Chapter 2), and so are adverbials. It is conceivable that a literary text could be written without any, although it would be rather stark. However in reality adverbials are extremely common. They are one of the main components of spontaneous speech, and this is one of the ways in which speech and writing really are rather different. Sentences written in Standard English have finite verbs, but conversation is constructed less in sentences and more in adverbials. Positioning adverbials allows writers to foreground or background material, and removing adverbials reveals the skeletal core of a text. Dividing them up into *how, where, why, when* allows you to see what the author has focussed on most.

15 On Clauses

1 Definition of term *clause*

A clause is the larger sense-unit surrounding a Verb Phrase. Clauses can be very short – co-extensive with the Verb Phrase – or longer, containing other elements.

Main clauses contain a finite verb and can stand alone (head verbs are marked in a darker shade):

[the chihuahua barked]MAIN

[the chihuahua was barking]MAIN

[It had been barking]MAIN

{ the chihuahua **barked** }
  Main Clause

{ the chihuahua **was** barking }
  Main Clause

{ It **had** been barking }
  Main Clause

Subordinate clauses have either a finite or nonfinite verb and cannot stand alone:

[whilst it was barking]SUB [the chihuahua pranced]MAIN

[the chihuahua barked]MAIN [where it stood]SUB

[prancing,]SUB, nonfinite [the chihuahua barked]MAIN

[the Chihuahua started]MAIN [to bark]SUB, nonfinite

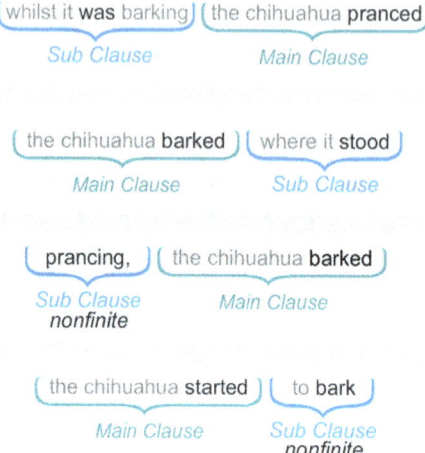

Subordinate clauses can be embedded in main clauses:

[the chihuahua] [that was barking]SUB [fell silent]MAIN

[the chihuahua] [which loved [to prance]]SUB, SUB [barked]MAIN

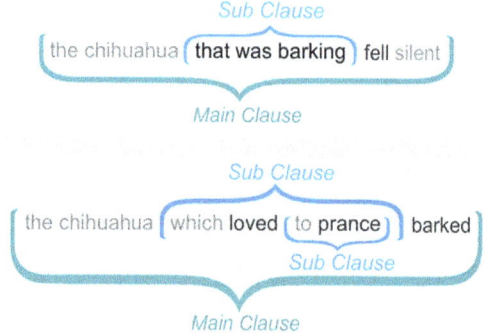

Main clauses can be strung together:

[the chihuahua pranced]MAIN and [barked]MAIN and [then fell silent]MAIN

There are three main coordinators linking main clause to main clause: *and, but, or*. However there are lots of subordinators linking subordinate clauses to main

clauses or other subordinate clauses. The main ones are *that*, and the *wh-* forms (more on these in Chapter 17):

[[As it skipped]SUB and yapped,]SUB] [the chihuahua] [[which was wearing a collar]SUB [studded with diamonds]SUB] [tangled its lead]MAIN and [fell over its owner's foot]MAIN

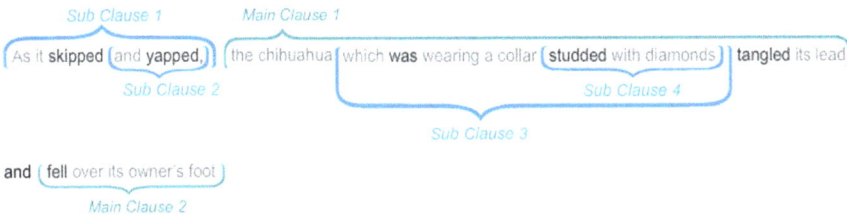

Notice how links don't always have to be explicit; in Standard English we can write *a collar studded with diamonds* or *a collar which was studded with diamonds*.

2 Demonstration of term *Clause Analysis*

Read through this fictional account of watching a silent film. It's an as-it-happens narrative, with the film related frame by frame. Spot the verbs, and see if you can figure out the clauses they sit in.

Just as we went into the cinema the lights went out and the screen flashed, 'Three-Fingered Kate, Episode 5. Lady Chichester's Necklace.'
    The piano began to play, sickly-sweet. Never again, never, not ever, never. Through caverns measureless to man down to a sunless sea. . . .
    The cinema smelt of poor people, and on the screen ladies and gentlemen in evening dress walked about with strained smiles.
    'There!' Ethel said, nudging. 'D'you see that girl – the one with the band round her hair? That's the one I know; that's my friend. Do you see? My God, isn't she terrible? My God, what a scream!' 'Oh, shut up,' somebody said. 'Shut up yourself,' Ethel said.
    I opened my eyes. On the screen a pretty girl was pointing a revolver at a group of guests. They backed away with their arms held high above their heads and expressions of terror on their faces. The pretty girl's lips moved. The fat hostess unclasped a necklace of huge pearls and fell, fainting, into the arms of a footman. The pretty girl, holding the revolver so that the audience could see that two of her fingers were missing, walked backwards towards the door. Her lips moved again.

You could see what she was saying. 'Keep 'em up. . . .' When the police appeared everybody clapped. When Three-Fingered Kate was caught everybody clapped louder still.

'Damned fools,' I said. 'Aren't they damned fools? Don't you hate them? They always clap in the wrong places and laugh in the wrong places.'

Jean Rhys, 1934, *Voyage in the Dark*

Here is the text again. Main clauses are in pink, subordinate clauses are in pale blue. I've highlighted the verb in each clause in darker shade.

[Just as we went into the cinema] [the lights went out] and [the screen flashed], 'Three-Fingered Kate, Episode 5. Lady Chichester's Necklace.'
 [The piano began to play, sickly-sweet.] Never again, never, not ever, never. Through caverns measureless to man down to a sunless sea. . . .
 [The cinema smelt of poor people], and [on the screen ladies and gentlemen in evening dress walked about with strained smiles.]
 ['There!' Ethel said], [nudging.] ['D'you see that girl – the one with the band round her hair?] [That's the one] [I know;] [that's my friend]. [Do you see?] [My God, isn't she terrible?] My God, what a scream!' ['Oh, shut up,'] [somebody said.] ['Shut up yourself,'] [Ethel said.]
 [I opened my eyes.] [On the screen a pretty girl was pointing a revolver at a group of guests.] [They backed away] [with their arms held high above their heads and expressions of terror on their faces.] [The pretty girl's lips moved.] [The fat hostess unclasped a necklace of huge pearls] and [fell], [fainting,] [into the arms of a footman.] [The pretty girl], [holding the revolver] [so that the audience could see] [that two of her fingers were missing,] [walked backwards towards the door.] [Her lips moved again.] [You could see] [what she was saying.] ['Keep 'em up. ....'] [When the police appeared] [everybody clapped.] [When Three-Fingered Kate was caught] [everybody clapped louder still.]
 ['Damned fools,' I said.] ['Aren't they damned fools?] [Don't you hate them?] [They always clap in the wrong places] and [laugh in the wrong places.']

In the first sentence there are two main clauses coordinated by *and*, and a subordinate clause. Try re-ordering: *the lights went out and the screen flashed just as we went into the cinema*. Or, *the screen flashed and the lights went out just as we went into the cinema*. Both *the lights went out* and *the screen flashed* can stand alone and so are main clauses, but *just as we went into the cinema* cannot.
 The title of the film has no verb and so it doesn't form a clause, nor does the quotation from Coleridge's *Kubla Khan* ("Through caverns measureless to man

down to a sunless sea") nor the sequence *never, ever, ever,* as the speaker reacts to the music, nor the exclamations *My God, what a scream!* When writing formal English prose, sentences with finite verbs are obligatory, but it's a different matter when people speak. Adverbials are the main unit of speech rather than clauses, and literary writing sometimes reflects this.

Main clauses are coordinated by *and* in this extract, and subordinate clauses are subordinated by just as, with, so that, that, what, when, when, and zero: *That's the one I know* has a missing subordinator. It could be rewritten as *That's the one whom I know,* or *That's the one who I know,* or *That's the one that I know.*

There are some embedded clauses: *fainting* is embedded in *fell into the arms of a footman,* and *the pretty girl walked backwards to the door* is interrupted by three embedded clauses.

There are some nonfinite *–ing* clauses, [nudging], [fainting], [holding the revolver]. These are called nonfinite clauses because *–ing* is not marked for number, person or tense.

The text is relatively heavy in main clauses, although not strikingly so. The finite verbs in the main clauses are: *went, flashed, began, smelt, walked, said, D' see, 's, 's, do see, is, shut, said, shut, said, opened, was pointing, backed, moved, unclasped, fell, walked, moved, could see, keep, clapped, clapped, said, are, Do hate, clap, laugh.* The verbs, finite and nonfinite, in the subordinate clauses are: *went, nudging, know, held, fainting, holding, could see, were missing, was saying, appeared, was caught.* In this particular extract, most of the simple past tense verbs sit in main clauses, and most of the auxiliaries and nonfinite *–ing* and *-ed* forms sit in subordinate clauses (this distribution is specific to this piece of writing; it's not always the case).

There is a distinction between the passages of dialogue and the description of the film. The dialogue is made up of short main clauses and is almost staccato. By contrast the description of the film contains subordinate clauses, nonfinite verbs and heavier Verb Phrases with a range of aspect. This enables the author to depict several things happening at once: the guests back off, look terrified and hold their hands up simultaneously. The girl walks backwards, threatens with the revolver, reveals her missing fingers to the audience and speaks, simultaneously. "Action packed", as a descriptor of this kind of film, had been coined by 1924 (*Oxford English Dictionary* action, *n.* C1.), but the Google Ngram Viewer (http://books.google.com/ngrams) reveals that films and books were rarely described this way in 1934. Instead of telling us that it was this kind of film, Rhys shows us.

3 Literary Exercise

Read through the following extract and analyse the clauses. What is the effect of the distribution of main and subordinate clauses?

Of course Eddie could drive, and he had a license and I didn't. Cowboy had two cars with him that he was driving back to Montana. His wife was at Grand Island, and he wanted us to drive one of the cars there, where she'd take over. At that point he was going north, and that would be the limit of our ride with him. But it was a good hundred miles into Nebraska, and of course we jumped for it. Eddie drove alone, the cowboy and myself following, and no sooner were we out of town than Eddie started to ball that jack ninety miles an hour out of sheer exuberance. "Damn me, what's that boy doing!" the cowboy shouted, and took off after him. It began to be like a race. For a minute I thought Eddie was trying to get away with the car — and for all I know that's what he meant to do. But the cowboy stuck to him and caught up with him and tooted the horn. Eddie slowed down. The cowboy tooted to stop. "Damn, boy, you're liable to get a flat going that speed. Can't you drive a little slower?"

"Well, I'll be damned, was I really going ninety?" said Eddie. "I didn't realize it on this smooth road."

"Just take it a little easy and we'll all get to Grand Island in one piece."

"Sure thing." And we resumed our journey. Eddie had calmed down and probably even got sleepy. So we drove a hundred miles across Nebraska, following the winding Platte with its verdant fields.

Jack Kerouak, 1957, *On the Road*

Here is the text again. Main clauses are in pink, subordinate clauses are in pale blue. I've highlighted the verb in each clause in darker colour.

[Of course Eddie could drive,] and [he had a license] and [I didn't.] [Cowboy had two cars with him] [that he was driving back to Montana.] [His wife was at Grand Island,] and [he wanted us] [to drive one of the cars there,] [where she'd take over.] [At that point he was going north,] and [that would be the limit of our ride with him.] But [it was a good hundred miles into Nebraska,] and [of course we jumped for it.] [Eddie drove alone,] [the cowboy and myself following,] and [no sooner were we out of town] than [Eddie started] [to ball that jack ninety miles an hour out of sheer exuberance.] ["Damn me,] [what's that boy doing!"] [the cowboy shouted,] and [took off after him.] [It began] [to be like a race.] [For a minute I thought] [Eddie was trying] [to get away with the car —] and [for all I know] [that's] [what he meant] [to do.] But [the cowboy stuck to him] and [caught up with him] and [tooted the horn.] [Eddie slowed down.] [The cowboy tooted] [to stop.] ["Damn, boy,] [you're liable] [to get a flat] [going that speed.] [Can't you drive a little slower?"]

["Well, I'll be damned,] [was I really going ninety?"] [said Eddie.] ["I didn't realize it on this smooth road."]

["Just take it a little easy] and [we'll all get to Grand Island in one piece."]

"Sure thing." And [we resumed our journey.] [Eddie had calmed down] and [probably even got sleepy.] [So we drove a hundred miles across Nebraska,] [following the winding Platte with its verdant fields.]

Analysis

In multiple-clause sentences, try re-ordering to discover which are main and which subordinate. Here's the sixth sentence re-ordered: *the cowboy and myself following, Eddie drove alone, and Eddie started to ball that jack ninety miles an hour out of sheer exuberance no sooner than we were out of town.* Re-ordering can give you a sense of emphasis: usually units at the start and units at the end will receive more emphasis than those in the middle. It is hard to remember things in the middle of a list. In the original, the emphasis is on Eddie's driving alone and his sheer exuberance, whereas in my re-ordering it would be the cowboy and myself, and being out of town. The sense remains the same, but it highlights how this text is focused on Eddie and his behaviour.

There is an elided subordinator in *For a minute I thought Eddie was trying to get away*: made explicit, it is *For a minute I thought that Eddie was trying to get away*.

As well as nonfinite *–ing* clauses, this text has nonfinite base-form clauses: to drive one of the cars, to ball that jack, to be like a race, to get away, to do, to stop, to get a flat. The base form is not marked for tense, person or number, and there's a considerable amount of incomplete actions here:

> *he wanted us to drive* (and it did in fact happen)
> *Eddie started to ball that jack* (and he continued to do so)
> *It began to be like a race* (and it continued to be so)
> *I thought Eddie was trying to get away* (but it turned out not to be so)
> *for all I know that's what he meant to do* (I'll never know)
> *The cowboy tooted to stop* (and he did)
> *you're liable to get a flat* (but he didn't)

Commentary

This use of subordinate clauses containing the base form builds a certain amount of suspense: as Eddie races off at ninety we share the speaker's concern, as neither the speaker nor the reader knows the outcome until the cowboy talks him down.

4 Teaching Point

To do clause analysis you need to be able to spot the verbs. Main clauses will have finite verbs, subordinate clauses may have finite or nonfinite ones. Clauses can come in any order. They are the larger units of the written sentence, and moving them around allows you to see where emphasis has originally been placed.

16 On Clauses: Coordinators and Subordinators

1 Definition of term *coordinators and subordinators*

Coordinators link units of equal status, either clauses or phrases [clauses contain a verb, whereas phrases do not, and main clauses can stand alone, whereas subordinate clauses cannot]. The principal coordinators are the conjunctions *and, but, or*. Subordinators link subordinate clauses to their hosts, and there are many of them: *if, since, although, whether, as, after, because, before, how, once, than, that, though, til, when, where, while . . .*

> [Columbus was an Italian] Main Clause and [he discovered America.] Main Clause
>
> [Columbus was an Italian] Main Clause but [he was sponsored by Spaniards.] Main Clause

Was it [the Nina] Noun Phrase or [the Santa Maria] Noun Phrase that was known as 'La Gallega'?

Coordinators

Subordinators

After returning from America, Columbus and his sons went to court over the profits.

If they had been given their share, they wouldn't have gone to court.

Columbus sailed to the Canaries, where he restocked his provisions.

Columbus discovered America, although he was seeking Cathay.

When a coordinator is present, it is known as syndetic coordination. When coordinators are absent, it is known as asyndetic coordination.

> Syndetic: Swiftly and safely, they sailed the Atlantic.

> Asyndetic: Swiftly, safely, they sailed the Atlantic.

2 Demonstration of term *coordinators and subordinators*

Read this poem, and spot how the clauses and phrases are linked together.

> **Columbus**
>
> Once upon a time there was an Italian,
> And some people thought he was a rapscallion,
> But he wasn't offended,
> Because other people thought he was splendid,
> And he said the world was round,
> And everybody made an uncomplimentary sound,
> But he went and tried to borrow some money from Ferdinand
> But Ferdinand said America was a bird in the bush and he'd rather have a berdinand,
> But Columbus' brain was fertile, it wasn't arid,
> And he remembered that Ferdinand was married,
> And he thought, there is no wife like a misunderstood one,
> Because if her husband thinks something is a terrible idea she is bound to think it a good one,
> So he perfumed his handkerchief with bay rum and citronella,
> And he went to see Isabella,
> And he looked wonderful but he had never felt sillier,
> And she said, I can't place the face but the aroma is familiar,
> And Columbus didn't say a word,
> All he said was, I am Columbus, the fifteenth-century Admiral Byrd,
> And, just as he thought, her disposition was very malleable,
> And she said, Here are my jewels, and she wasn't penurious like Cornelia the mother of the Gracchi, she wasn't referring to her children, no, she was referring to her jewels, which were very very valuable,
> So Columbus said, Somebody show me the sunset and somebody did and he set sail for it,
> And he discovered America and they put him in jail for it,
> And the fetters gave him welts,
> And they named America after somebody else,

So the sad fate of Columbus ought to be pointed out to every child and every voter,
Because it has a very important moral, which is, Don't be a discoverer, be a promoter.

Ogden Nash, 1938, *Columbus*

Here is the poem again, with the coordinators which link independent clauses together in red, subordinators which link host and subordinate clauses together in blue, and mauve and green for phrasal coordinators and subordinators.

1 Once upon a time there was an Italian,
2 And some people thought he was a rapscallion,
3 But he wasn't offended,
4 Because other people thought he was splendid,
5 And he said the world was round,
6 And everybody made an uncomplimentary sound,
7 But he went and tried to borrow some money from Ferdinand
8 But Ferdinand said America was a bird in the bush and he'd rather have a berdinand,
9 But Columbus' brain was fertile, it wasn't arid,
10 And he remembered that Ferdinand was married,
11 And he thought, there is no [wife like a misunderstood one],
12 Because if her husband thinks something is a terrible idea she is bound to think it a good one,
13 So he perfumed his handkerchief with [bay rum and citronella],
14 And he went to see Isabella,
15 And he looked wonderful but he had never felt sillier,
16 And she said, I can't place the face but the aroma is familiar,
17 And Columbus didn't say a word,
18 All he said was, I am Columbus, the fifteenth-century Admiral Byrd,
19 And, just as he thought, her disposition was very malleable,
20 And she said, Here are my jewels, and she wasn't [penurious like Cornelia] the mother of the Gracchi, she wasn't referring to her children, no, she was referring to her jewels, which were very very valuable,
21 So Columbus said, Somebody show me the sunset and somebody did and he set sail for it,
22 And he discovered America and they put him in jail for it,
23 And the fetters gave him welts,
24 And they named America after somebody else,
25 So the sad fate of Columbus ought to be pointed out to [every child and every voter],
26 Because it has a very important moral, which is, Don't be a discoverer, be a promoter.

The humour in this poem owes a good deal to its formal qualities: the pairing end-rhyme, coupled with the stretching of the metre. There's an obvious cleverness about rhyme, and Ogden Nash was a talented rhymester. During his lifetime (1904–1971) his work was popular and known as 'light verse'. Light verse needs just as much crafting as the weightier sort; the poem is mainly hung together by means of coordinating conjunctions, and the stretching of the metre in lines 20 and 21 works against the default backdrop of the many short coordinated main clauses. Children are usually taught not to use multiple *and*s in close proximity because children learn subordinate clauses late in their development, so that lots of main clauses all linked by *and* sounds immature. The cleverness of the rhyme-scheme, and the pragmatics of Columbus's cunning, are juxtaposed against the simplicity of the coordinated short main clauses. The incongruity amuses.

3 Literary Exercise

Find the coordinators and subordinators in the text below, and consider their purpose in the text.

It was a city asleep and deathly silent in the emptiness of the night and Titus rose to his feet and trembled as he saw it, not only with the cold but with astonishment that while he had slept, and while he had drawn the marks in the dust, and while he had watched the beetle, this city should have been there all the time and that a turn of his head might have filled his eyes with the domes and spires of silver; with shimmering slums; with parks and arches and a threading river. And all upon the flanks of a great mountain, hoary with forests.

But as he stared at the high slopes of the city his feelings were not those of a child or a youth, nor of an adult with romantic leanings. His responses were no longer clear and simple, for he had been through much since he had escaped from Ritual, and he was no longer child or youth, but by reason of his knowledge of tragedy, violence and the sense of his own perfidy, he was far more than these, though less than *man*.

Kneeling there he seemed most lost. Lost in the bright grey night. Lost in his separation. Lost in a swath of space in which the city lay like one-thing, secure in its cohesion, a great moon-bathed creature that throbbed in its sleep as from a single pulse.

Mervyn Peake, 1959, *Titus Alone*

Here is the text again, with the coordinators which link independent clauses together in red, subordinators which link host and subordinate clauses together in blue: strong colours indicate clauses, pale colours indicate phrases.

It was a city [asleep and deathly silent] in the emptiness of the night and Titus rose to his feet and trembled as he saw it, [not only with the cold but with astonishment] that while he had slept, and while he had drawn the marks in the dust, and while he had watched the beetle, this city should have been there all the time and that a turn of his head might have filled his eyes with the [domes and spires] of silver; with shimmering slums; with [parks and arches and a threading river. And all] upon the flanks of a great mountain, hoary with forests.

But as he stared at the high slopes of the city his feelings were not those of [a child or a youth, nor of an adult] with romantic leanings. His responses were no longer [clear and simple], for he had been through much since he had escaped from Ritual, and he was no longer [child or youth], but by reason of his knowledge of [tragedy, violence and the sense of his own perfidy], he was [far more than these, though less than *man*].

Kneeling there he seemed most lost. Lost in the bright grey night. Lost in his separation. Lost in a swath of space in which [the city lay like one-thing], secure in its cohesion, a great moon-bathed creature that [throbbed in its sleep as from a single pulse].

Analysis

By contrast with Ogden Nash's text, no single connective form predominates. Peake uses coordinators and subordinators in more or less the same amounts. He also uses asyndetic coordination:

> Kneeling there he seemed most lost. Lost in the bright grey night. Lost in his separation. Lost in a swath of space in which the city lay like one-thing . . .

Don't be mislead by the punctuation here; there is only one finite verb (*seemed*). We can repunctuate this as: "Kneeling there he seemed most lost: lost in the bright grey night, lost in his separation, lost in a swath of space in which the city lay like one-thing." We can supply the elided clause and phrase connectives as: "Kneeling there he seemed most lost: [lost in the bright grey night] and [lost in his separation] and [lost in a swath of space] in which the city lay like one-thing." Nor is this the only repetition:

> while he had slept, and while he had drawn the marks in the dust, and while he had watched the beetle . . .

And there is also repetition of the preposition *with* in the series of coordinated phrases:

> with the [domes and spires] of silver; with shimmering slums; with [parks and arches and a threading river. And all]

Commentary

The cumulative effect of so many coordinated and subordinated clauses and repetition is rhetorical, befitting the semantic content, which is of the young Titus maturing as a result of experience and duress. For some readers, the effect will be dramatic. For others, the effect will be more one of melodrama, perhaps even sententiousness (*Oxford English Dictionary* sententious *adj.* 3. 'affectedly or pompously formal').

4 Teaching Point

Coordinators alone tend to make a text sound simple; a multiplicity of subordinators will make a text sound complex.

Identifying clause and phrase connectors is all part of clause analysis. Typically, it is hard to do at first, but you get better at it the more you practice. If you can analyse clauses correctly you can be confident of the underpinnings of a text.

17 On Clauses: Relative Pronouns

1 Definition of term *Relative Pronouns*

Relative pronouns link main clauses to a type of subordinate clause known as a relative clause. They are easy to remember: *wh-* forms and *that*:

Relative pronouns   that, which, who, whose, whom, where, when, how, zero (0)

The plane that was empty took off.
The plane which was full landed.
The passenger who was hungry strapped herself in.
The passenger whose meal was non-vegetarian complained.
The passengers for whom flying was an everyday concern fell asleep.
The plane is flying where the sun is shining.
The loads need to be redistributed when the plane is flying empty.
We were wondering how the plane stays up.
The passengers 0 we sat next to told us.

Here are the relative pronouns and the clauses they govern. Main clauses can stand alone, whereas subordinate clauses don't make sense on their own.

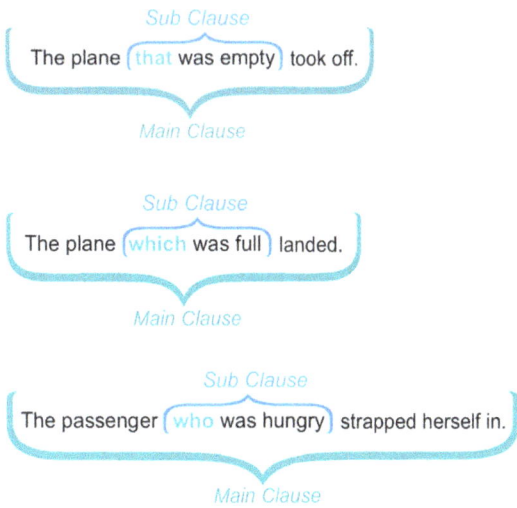

Wh- forms can also be used for questions, in which case they are known as interrogative pronouns: Which? Who? Whose? Whom? Where? When? How?

2 Demonstration of *Relative Pronouns*

The following extract is written by a Hawai'ian author, using a combination of Hawai'ian Creole English (known as *pidgin* in Hawai'i), American English and Standard English.

Note on dialect: in Hawai'ian Creole English *wen* is a past-tense marker in the Verb Phrase [*wen* + base form]: *wen make* 'made', *wen decide* 'decided'.

At first wuz go, den no go, den go again. My maddah wen make my faddahs take one physical last month wen we wuz planning dis trip and I guess da doc toll him he bettah lay off da cigs cuz my Poppa Puff used to smoke like two packs a day and now he no smoke nahting. He get couple pills he gotta take too, but dey no like tell me wot ees fo'. My maddah wuz all worried if he could handles going on dis trip, but he sed no mattah wot he wuz going.

My maddah da one always flip-flopping. Jus like wen she drive. To moss people, one yellow light mean slow down, cuss, slow down. To my maddah, one yellow light mean stop, go-stop, ah mo beddah GO I tink so. In da end, my maddah wen decide fo' stay home save money. Gotta tink da future she sed, plus she had fo' watch my kid bruddah. So wuz jus me and my faddahs on dis plane ride.

Usually me and my faddahs no talk nahting. Not dat we hate each oddahs. Jus we no mo' nahting fo' say. My maddah da one get da motor mout, talking on and on to da endless power kine. My faddah sez her mout only good fo' complain, complain about how everyting so expensive nowadays – I dunno why, but only recently my maddah sez cannot afford da kine Kellogs Cereal Variety Packs. Get mo' bang fo' your buck she sez if we buy one big box of generic, look like, but not Cheerios and so I gotta eat 'em everyday fo' da whole month until by da end of da first week da fake Cheerios no seem so cheery anymo', but too bad so sad fo' me cuz das all I getting, cuz das all get, and das all I going get, until I finish dat big buffo bargain size box.

My faddah sez da plane ride going take only like twenny-thirty minutes. And dis flight attendant stewardess-man is jus one rude dude, cuss. Ees like he tink I looking him wot, so he looking me why, only I not looking him wot, I looking him, I THIRSTY WEA MY DRINK, cuss. My troat stay all dehydronated. At least I practice da kine good kine mannahsrisms at my house. Cannot be rude, cuss. Wen all my friends come ova, da first ting I do is offah dem drink and someting to eat. "Ryan, Kyle, you guys like Cheerios? Now hurry up eat 'em befo' my maddah see."

Lee A. Tonouchi, 2001, *da mayor of lahaina*

Here is the text again, with the relative pronouns in green, the interrogative pronouns in blue, and zero relative pronouns marked with a zero symbol.

At first wuz go, den no go, den go again. My maddah wen make my faddahs take one physical last month wen we wuz planning dis trip and I guess 0 da doc toll him 0 he bettah lay off da cigs cuz my Poppa Puff used to smoke like two packs a day and now he no smoke nahting. He get couple pills 0 he gotta take too, but dey no like tell me wot ees fo'. My maddah wuz all worried if he could handles going on dis trip, but he sed 0 no mattah wot he wuz going.

My maddah da one 0 always flip-flopping. Jus like wen she drive. To moss people, one yellow light mean slow down, cuss, slow down. To my maddah, one yellow light mean stop, go-stop, ah mo beddah GO I tink so. In da end, my maddah wen decide fo' stay home save money. Gotta tink da future she sed, plus she had fo' watch my kid bruddah. So wuz jus me and my faddahs on dis plane ride.

Usually me and my faddahs no talk nahting. Not dat we hate each oddahs. Jus 0 we no mo' nahting fo' say. My maddah da one 0 get da motor mout, talking on and on to da endless power kine. My faddah sez 0 her mout only good fo' complain, complain about how everyting so expensive nowadays – I dunno why, but only recently my maddah sez 0 cannot afford da kine Kellogs Cereal Variety Packs. Get mo' bang fo' your buck she sez if we buy one big box of generic, look like, but not Cheerios and so I gotta eat 'em everyday fo' da whole month until by da end of da first week da fake Cheerios no seem so cheery anymo', but too bad so sad fo' me cuz das all 0 I getting, cuz das all 0 get, and das all 0 I going get, until I finish dat big buffo bargin size box.

My faddah sez 0 da plane ride going take only like twenny-thirty minutes. And dis flight attendant stewardess-man is jus one rude dude, cuss. Ees like he tink 0 I looking him wot, so he looking me why, only I not looking him wot, I looking him, I THIRSTY WEA MY DRINK, cuss. My troat stay all dehydrated. At least I practice da kine good kine mannahsrisms at my house. Cannot be rude, cuss. Wen all my friends come ova, da first ting 0 I do is offah dem drink and someting to eat. "Ryan, Kyle, you guys like Cheerios? Now hurry up eat 'em befo' my maddah see."

last month [wen we wuz planning dis trip]: 'last month when we were planning this trip]'

I guess [0 da doc toll him]: 'I guess that the doc told him'

[0 he bettah lay off da cigs]: 'that he better lay off the cigs'

He get couple pills [0 he gotta take]: 'He got a couple of pills that he's got to take'

dey no like tell me [wot ees fo']: 'they didn't want to tell me what it's for' or 'they haven't, like, told me what it's for'

he sed [0 no mattah wot he wuz going] 'he said that no matter what (happened) he was going' – *what* in this context is a nominal relative pronoun

My maddah da one [0 always flip-flopping]: 'My mother is the one who is always flip-flopping'

Jus like [wen she drive]: 'Just like when she drives'

[Not dat we hate each oddahs]: '(It is) not that we hate each other'

Jus [0 we no mo' nahting fo' say]: '(It's) just that we've nothing much to say'

My maddah da one [0 get da motor mout]: 'My mother is the one who has the motor mouth'

My faddah sez [0 her mout only good fo' complain, complain]: 'My father says that her mouth is only good for complaining'

about [how everyting so expensive]: 'about how everything (is) so expensive'

I dunno why: 'I don't know why'

my maddah sez [0 cannot afford da kine Kellogs Cereal Variety Packs]: 'my mother says that we cannot afford those Kellogs Cereal Variety Packs'

[das all] [0 I getting]: 'that's all that I'm getting'

[cuz das all] [0 get]: 'because that's all that (we've) got'

and [das all] [0 I going get]: 'and that's all that I'm going (to) get'

My faddah sez [0 da plane ride going take only like twenny-thirty minutes]: 'My father says that the plane ride (is) going (to) take only like twenty-thirty minutes'

Ees like he tink [0 I looking him]: '(It)'s like he thinks that I'm looking (at) him'

I looking him wot: 'I'm looking at him: what!'

so he looking me why: 'so he's looking at me: why?'

I not looking him wot: 'I'm not looking at him: what!'

WEA MY DRINK: 'where's my drink?'

[Wen all my friends come ova], da first ting [0 I do]: 'When all my friends come over, the first thing that I do'

Note: In *dat big buffo bargin size box*, 'that' is a determiner.

Although there may have been unfamiliar grammatical and lexical material which caused you momentary processing difficulties, it's unlikely that the relative pronouns, or zero relative pronouns, caused you much trouble. If relative pronouns are the object of the relative clause, they can be omitted, and although plenty were omitted in Tonouchi's text, they could be omitted in those positions in Standard English too. In many dialects (although not Standard English), relative pronouns can also be omitted when they are the subject of the relative clause, as in *My maddah da one 0 always flip-flopping*. Here's the title of a song written by Kirsty MacColl and Philip Rambow:

There's a guy works down the chip shop swears he's Elvis

'There's a guy (who) works down the chip shop (who) swears (that) he's Elvis'

The two *who*s are the subject of the following relative clause. This won't work in all dialects, but it's possible in Hawai'ian Creole English and London English.

Being *that*ful, putting in all the relative pronouns, makes a text sound more formal. Leaving them out makes it sound more like speech.

3 Literary Exercise

Identify the relative pronouns in the following poem. What is their effect?

I'r Hen Iaith A'i Chaneuon

*If the tongue spoke only the mind's truth,
there wouldn't be any neighbours.*
- The Red Book of Hergest

When I go down to Wales for the long bank holiday
to visit my wife's grandfather, who is teetotal,
who is a non-smoker, who does not approve
of anyone who is not teetotal and a non-smoker,
when I go down to Wales for the long, long bank holiday
with my second wife to visit her grandfather
who deserted Methodism for The Red Flag,
who won't hear a word against Stalin,
who despite my oft-professed socialism
secretly believes I am still with the Pope's legions,
receiving coded telegrams from the Vatican
specifying the dates, times and positions I should adopt
for political activity and sexual activity,
who in his ninetieth year took against boxing,
which was the only thing I could ever talk to him about,
when I visit my second wife's surviving grandfather,
and when he listens to the football results in Welsh,

I will sometimes slip out to the pub.

I will sometimes slip out to the pub
and drink pint upon pint of that bilious whey
they serve there, where the muzak will invariably be
'The Best of the Rhosllanerchrugog Male Voice Choir'
and I will get trapped by some brain donor from up the valley
who will really talk about "the language so strong and so beautiful
that has grown out of the ageless mountains,
that speech of wondrous beauty that our fathers wrought,"
who will chant to me in Welsh his soporific verses
about Gruffydd ap Llywelyn and Daffydd ap Llywelyn,
and who will give me two solid hours of slaver
because I don't speak Irish, and who will then bring up religion,
then I will tell him I know one Irish prayer about a Welsh king
on that very subject, and I will recite for him as follows:
'Fág uaim do eaglais ghallda
Is do chreideamh gan bonn gan bhrí,
Mar gurb é is cloch bonn dóibh
Magairle Anraoi Rí.' 'Beautiful,'
he will say, as they all do, 'It sounds quite beautiful.'

Ian Duhig, 1991, *I'r Hen Iaith A'i Chaneuon*

Notes on the poem:
1. *I'r Hen Iaith A'i Chaneuon* ('To the Old Tongue and its Songs') is the Welsh title of a poem by Walter Dowding.
2. The Irish verse is by Antoine Ó Reachtabhra, and translates roughly as:

'Away with your foreign religion,
And your baseless, meaningless faith,
For the only rock it is built upon
Is the bollocks of King Henry the Eighth.'

3. The poet Ian Duhig is a Londoner of Irish ancestry. Do not confuse the poet with the narrator here: the poem does not represent Ian Duhig's own views of Welsh people, Welsh-language speakers or their country.

Here are the relative pronouns and zero relative pronouns in green.

When I go down to Wales for the long bank holiday
to visit my wife's grandfather, who is teetotal,
who is a non-smoker, who does not approve
of anyone who is not teetotal and a non-smoker,
when I go down to Wales for the long, long bank holiday
with my second wife to visit her grandfather,
who deserted Methodism for The Red Flag,
who won't hear a word against Stalin,

who despite my oft-professed socialism
secretly believes 0 I am still with the Pope's legions,
receiving coded telegrams from the Vatican
specifying the dates, times and positions 0 I should adopt
for political activity and sexual activity,
who in his ninetieth year took against boxing,
which was the only thing 0 I could ever talk to him about,
when I visit my second wife's surviving grandfather,
and when he listens to the football results in Welsh,
I will sometimes slip out to the pub.

    I will sometimes slip out to the pub
and drink pint upon pint of that bilious whey
0 they serve there, where the muzak will invariably be
'The Best of the Rhosllanerchrugog Male Voice Choir'
and I will get trapped by some brain donor from up the valley
who will really talk about "the language so strong and so beautiful
that has grown out of the ageless mountains,
that speech of wondrous beauty that our fathers wrought,"
who will chant to me in Welsh his soporific verses
about Gruffydd ap Llywelyn and Daffydd ap Llywelyn,
and who will give me two solid hours of slaver
because I don't speak Irish, and who will then bring up religion,
then I will tell him 0 I know one Irish prayer about a Welsh king
on that very subject, and I will recite for him as follows:
'Fág uaim do eaglais ghallda
Is do chreideamh gan bonn gan bhrí,
Mar gurb é is cloch bonn dóibh
Magairle Anraoi Rí.' 'Beautiful,'
he will say, as they all do, 'It sounds quite beautiful.'

Analysis

Everything that precedes the last line of the first stanza is subordinate to the main clause *I will sometimes slip out to the pub*. (Try placing the main clause at the beginning: 'I will sometimes slip out to the pub / When I go down to Wales for the long bank holiday . . . and when he listens to the football results in Welsh' – all the clauses are dependent on it.)

Commentary

The first stanza is about all the many things the Welsh grandfather is against, as a result of which the narrator cannot find much in common with him, and the sixteen relative clauses before getting to the point where he can slip out to the pub demonstrate his boredom.

The second stanza is also about the narrator's boredom, this time in the pub, listening to a Welsh patriot who values the Welsh language for symbolic and sentimental reasons. The rude Irish verse doesn't merit 'Beautiful,' . . . 'It sounds quite beautiful'; but this is the standard response the narrator receives from Celtic patriots who don't understand Irish Gaelic to anything in Irish Gaelic.

4 Teaching Point

Relative pronouns are linking devices, linking subordinate relative clauses to main clauses. Relative pronouns are easily remembered (*that* and *wh-* forms); less easy to spot are the zero relative pronouns. They are very common, and cause a text to sound less formal.

18 -*ing* forms

1 Definition of term –*ing forms*

There are several kinds of –*ing* forms, which sit in both the Noun Phrase and the Verb Phrase:

Verb Phrase		*I am singing.*
		I might have been singing.
Non-finite –*ing* clause		*I skipped down the steps, singing.*
		Singing, I skipped down the steps.
Noun Phrase	noun	*This singing is heavenly.*
	adjective	*That echoing song.*

Certain nouns were formed from verbs, and have fossilized in the –*ing* form: the *railings*, a *building*, a *gathering*, the *morning*, a *helping*, the *stockings*, a *walloping*

Certain adjectives have formed from verbs in the –*ing* form: a *thundering* wallop, a *heaving* sea, a *flying* ponytail, in a *blinding* flash, in the *pouring* rain, a *freezing* winter

Certain adverbs can be formed from –*ing* forms: *overarchingly* helpful manners, *eye-wateringly* high prices, *trouser-splittingly* funny, *toe-curlingly* excruciating

An echoing gathering, groaning with nail-scrapingly excruciating wailing, was flailingly warbling from morning to evening – authors won't usually stack up the –*ing* forms to quite this density, but as you can see, -*ing* is versatile.

You may know the –*ing* form when used in the verb phrase as a 'present participle'. There's nothing wrong with this label but linguists use the term –*ing* form because the gradations between Verb Phrase use and Noun Phrase use can be fuzzy. Consider the gerund (a nouny kind of –*ing* form derived from a verb):

To John Curlow for digging a ditch – £10

This could be made more explicitly nouny, by preceding it with the definite article *the*:

To John Curlow for the digging of a ditch – £10

or less nouny, where like a verb it is followed by a direct object alone:

To John Curlow digging a ditch – £10

Notice that when sitting in the Verb Phrase, the *–ing* form is not marked for person, tense or number, and is therefore not finite. It is the auxiliary verb which carries these markers: *I am singing, you are singing, we were singing*. *–ing* forms can function as the verb in non-finite clauses: *Singing loudly is fun; seeing is believing.*

2 Demonstration of *–ing* forms

The following text is written in a mixture of Standard English, London English and East Caribbean English. East Caribbean dialects typically omit the auxiliary verb in Verb Phrases taking the *–ing* form: *I going*, where Standard English has *I am/was going*. They also use the subject pronoun in object position (*telling she* where Standard English has *telling her*), don't mark the third-person singular *–s* (*he make haste*), and certain words are used in different senses to those of Standard English: *yard* 'home', *to full* 'to fill'. Read the text and look out for the *-ing* forms.

The summer night descend with stars, they walking hand in hand, and Galahad feeling hearts.
   'It was a lovely evening –' Daisy began.
   'Come and go in the yard,' Galahad say.
   'What?' Daisy say.
   'The yard. Where I living.'
   All this time he was stalling, because he feeling sort of shame to bring the girl in that old basement room, but if the date end in fiasco he know the boys would never finish giving him tone for spending all that money and not eating.
   Daisy start to hesitate but he make haste and catch a number twelve, telling she that it all on the way home. When they hop off by the Water she was still getting on prim, but Galahad know was only grandcharge, and besides the old blood getting hot, so he walk Daisy brisk down the road, and she quiet as a mouse. They went down the basement steps and Galahad fumble for the key, and when he open the door a whiff of stale food and old clothes and dampness and dirt come out the door and he only waiting to hear what Daisy would say.
   But she ain't saying nothing, and he walk through the passage and open the door and put the light on.
   Daisy sit down on the bed and Galahad say: 'You want a cup of char?' And without waiting for any answer he full the pot in the tap and put it on the ring and turn the gas on. He feel so excited that he had to light a cigarette, and he keep saying Take it easy to himself.
   'Is this your room?' Daisy say, looking around and shifting about as if she restless.

'Yes,' Galahad say. 'You like it?'

'Yes,' Daisy say.

Galahad throw a copy of *Ebony* to her and she begin to turn the pages.

With all the excitement Galahad taking off the good clothes carefully and slowly, putting the jacket and trousers on the hanger right away, and folding up the shirt and putting it in the drawer.

When the water was boiling he went to the cupboard and take out a packet of tea, and he shake some down in the pot.

Daisy look at him as if he mad.

'Is that how you make tea?' she ask.

'Yes,' Galahad say. 'No foolishness about it. Tea is tea – you just drop some in the kettle. If you want it strong, you drop plenty. If you want it weak, you drop little bit. And so you make a lovely cuppa.'

He take the kettle off and rest it on a sheet of *Daily Express* on the ground. He bring two cups, a spoon, a bottle of milk and a packet of sugar.

'Fix up,' he say, handing Daisy a cup.

They sit down there sipping the tea and talking.

'You get that raise the foreman was promising you?' Galahad ask, for something to say.

'What did you say? You know it will take me some time to understand everything you say. The way you West Indians speak!'

'What wrong with it?' Galahad ask. 'Is English we speaking.'

And so he coasting a little oldtalk until the tea finish, and afterwards he start to make one set of love to Daisy.

'It was battle royal in that basement, man,' he tell Moses afterwards, and he went on to give a lot of detail, though all of that is nothing to a old veteran like Moses, is only to Galahad is new because is the first time with a white number. Moses smile a knowing smile, a tired smile, and 'Take it easy,' he tell Sir Galahad.

Sam Selvon, 1956, *The Lonely Londoners*

Here is the text again with the *–ing* forms made explicit, with Noun Phrase *–ing* forms in mauve and Verb Phrase *–ing* forms in light blue. Non-finite *–ing* clauses are marked in dark blue.

The summer night descend with stars, they walking hand in hand, and Galahad feeling hearts.

'It was a lovely evening –' Daisy began.

'Come and go in the yard,' Galahad say.

'What?' Daisy say.

'The yard. Where I living.'

All this time he was stalling, because he feeling sort of shame to bring the girl in that old basement room, but if the date end in fiasco he know the boys would never finish giving him tone for spending all that money and not eating.

Daisy start to hesitate but he make haste and catch a number twelve, telling she that it all on the way home. When they hop off by the Water she was still getting on prim, but Galahad know was only grandcharge, and besides the old blood getting hot, so he walk Daisy brisk down the road, and she quiet as a mouse. They went down the basement steps and Galahad fumble for the key, and when he open the door a whiff of stale food and old clothes and dampness and dirt come out the door and he only waiting to hear what Daisy would say.

But she ain't saying nothing, and he walk through the passage and open the door and put the light on.

Daisy sit down on the bed and Galahad say: 'You want a cup of char?' And without waiting for any answer he full the pot in the tap and put it on the ring and turn the gas on. He feel so excited that he had to light a cigarette, and he keep saying Take it easy to himself.

'Is this your room?' Daisy say, looking around and shifting about as if she restless.

'Yes,' Galahad say. 'You like it?'

'Yes,' Daisy say.

Galahad throw a copy of *Ebony* to her and she begin to turn the pages.

With all the excitement Galahad taking off the good clothes carefully and slowly, putting the jacket and trousers on the hanger right away, and folding up the shirt and putting it in the drawer.

When the water was boiling he went to the cupboard and take out a packet of tea, and he shake some down in the pot.

Daisy look at him as if he mad.

'Is that how you make tea?' she ask.

'Yes,' Galahad say. 'No foolishness about it. Tea is tea – you just drop some in the kettle. If you want it strong, you drop plenty. If you want it weak, you drop little bit. And so you make a lovely cuppa.'

He take the kettle off and rest it on a sheet of *Daily Express* on the ground. He bring two cups, a spoon, a bottle of milk and a packet of sugar.

'Fix up,' he say, handing Daisy a cup.

They sit down there sipping the tea and talking.

'You get that raise the foreman was promising you?' Galahad ask, for something to say.

'What did you say? You know it will take me some time to understand everything you say. The way you West Indians speak!'

'What wrong with it?' Galahad ask. 'Is English we speaking.'

And so he coasting a little oldtalk until the tea finish, and afterwards he start to make one set of love to Daisy.

'It was battle royal in that basement, man,' he tell Moses afterwards, and he went on to give a lot of detail, though all of that is nothing to a old veteran like Moses, is only to Galahad is new because is the first time with a white number. Moses smile a knowing smile, a tired smile, and 'Take it easy,' he tell Sir Galahad.

I have allocated the *–ing* forms according to whether they can more easily be preceded by *the* (*the evening*), in which case they sit in the Noun Phrase; or by a verb ((*were*) *walking*, (*was*) *feeling*, (*am*) *living*), or by a clause (*telling, waiting*), in which case they are Verb Phrase usages. You will have noticed that both Galahad and the narrator do use some Standard English tensed [aux V + *–ing*]: *he was stalling, she was getting on, the water was boiling, the foreman was promising*. Galahad has been living in his Bayswater bedsitter for a while at this point, and both he and his narrator can switch into Standard English, and also use some more local London English forms (*a lovely cuppa*). (Selvon himself was a Londoner from Trinidad, and used Standard English in other publications.) Although at first sight there seem to be a lot of *–ing* forms in this text, most of them sit in the Verb Phrase and act as continuous past-tense usage. The text comprises a series of small domestic actions – entering the bedsit, taking off day-clothes, lighting the gas, fetching and making tea, talking, sipping – as Galahad, feeling hearts, leads up to his seduction of the complicit Daisy.

3 Literary Exercise

Analyse the *–ing* forms in the following text. Why do you think they cluster where they do?

Bertie, looking in that evening, found her halfway through a bottle of Sancerre, calm in her white silk shirt and her patterned velvet skirt.

'You must spend a fortune on that stuff,' he said uneasily. 'And it can't be doing you any good.' He hated evidence of solitary habits, just as he hated the echoing silence of the flat, as he stood outside wondering whether or not to use his old key.

'Don't worry,' said Blanche. 'I have never been drunk in my life. You do not run the risk of seeing me hanging round a lamppost with a riotous hat over one eye. I think you are frightened of my turning up at your house and making a scene. Bursting in on your guests while Mousie is dishing up the stuffed peppers. Having to be removed by men in white coats. Reduced to begging in the streets, asking passers-by for five pounds for a cup of tea. Yourself shuddering with disgust on the other side of the road. Anyway, I can afford it. That must be one worry off your mind.'

Bertie sat down in his usual chair with a slight sigh.

'I hope I find you well,' said Blanche, looking at him with an expression of some reserve.

Bertie appeared strange to her. Mousie insisted that in the evenings and at weekends he changed into clothes that broadcast messages of youth and leisure. He was like a child, Blanche thought. 'In any case, I think it behoves lonely women to take on the burden of the world's drinking,' she said. 'Curious verb, behoves. I behove, you behove. Or is it intransitive? You'll find a bottle of Malaga in the larder,' she added, seeing that, as usual, he was taking no notice. 'Or there's some Madeira, if you prefer it. With a sliver of Madeira cake, perhaps.'

Bertie ran a finger round where his collar ought to be. 'Home-made?' he enquired, remembering that he was wearing a polo-necked jersey.

'Naturally,' said Blanche, getting up and going out for the tray.

Anita Brookner, 1986, *A Misalliance*

Here is the text again with the *–ing* forms made explicit, with Noun Phrase *–ing* forms in mauve and Verb Phrase *–ing* forms in light blue. Non-finite *–ing* clauses are marked in dark blue.

Bertie, looking in that evening, found her halfway through a bottle of Sancerre, calm in her white silk shirt and her patterned velvet skirt.

'You must spend a fortune on that stuff,' he said uneasily. 'And it can't be doing you any good.' He hated evidence of solitary habits, just as he hated the echoing silence of the flat, as he stood outside wondering whether or not to use his old key.

'Don't worry,' said Blanche. 'I have never been drunk in my life. You do not run the risk of seeing me hanging round a lamppost with a riotous hat over one eye. I think you are frightened of my turning up at your house and making a scene. Bursting in on your guests while Mousie is dishing up the stuffed peppers. Having to be removed by men in white coats. Reduced to begging in the streets, asking passers-by for five pounds for a cup of tea. Yourself shuddering with disgust on the other side of the road. Anyway, I can afford it. That must be one worry off your mind.'

Bertie sat down in his usual chair with a slight sigh.

'I hope I find you well,' said Blanche, looking at him with an expression of some reserve.

Bertie appeared strange to her. Mousie insisted that in the evenings and at weekends he changed into clothes that broadcast messages of youth and leisure. He was like a child, Blanche thought. 'In any case, I think it behoves lonely women to take on the burden of the world's drinking,' she said. 'Curious verb, behoves. I behove, you behove. Or is it intransitive? You'll find a bottle of Malaga in the larder,' she added, seeing that, as usual, he was taking no notice. 'Or there's some Madeira, if you prefer it. With a sliver of Madeira cake, perhaps.'

Bertie ran a finger round where his collar ought to be. 'Home-made?' he enquired, remembering that he was wearing a polo-necked jersey.

'Naturally,' said Blanche, getting up and going out for the tray.

Analysis

I have allocated the *–ing* forms according to whether they can more easily be preceded by *the* (*the evening, the world's drinking*) or *my* (*my making a scene, my bursting in*), in which case they sit in the Noun Phrase; or by a verb (*it can't be doing, Mousie is dishing up*), or by a clause (*she added, seeing; he enquired, remembering*), in which case they are Verb Phrase usages.

Commentary

Blanche is not talking about factual matters anchored in the past, present or future. Rather, she's empathising with Bertie, imagining that he's worried about her being jealous of Mousie and expressing that jealousy in public. And then having said as much, she extends and elaborates the theme for six extra *–ing* forms (*bursting, dishing, having, begging, asking, shuddering*) (she also goes off at a tangent later when she ponders the word *behove*). The *–ing* form, being non-finite, conveys the non-factual, non-temporal aspect of her fantasy, which is only slimly based in reality. Blanche is not wittering, exactly, there is a logic to her progression, but the first two (*seeing, hanging*) conveyed her point; there was no need to continue. From *seeing* to *shuddering*, Blanche is not directly engaging with Bertie as he is in the here and now, but rather her projected view of how she and he might hypothetically behave, and so Bertie pays little attention. The phrase 'as usual' lets us know that Blanche habitually expresses her ideas to excess (she has 'a fertile imagination' in common parlance) and, accordingly, Bertie habitually ignores them. *–ing* is a useful device for avoiding specifics.

4 Teaching Point

There are several different kinds of *–ing* form, all common, and none of which are finite. It is usual for authors to use plenty of them, and by and large, they are not particularly noticeable. If you find a predominance of *–ing* forms, or one sort of *–ing* form only, then it's worth asking why the author chose to use them.

19 On Anaphora

1 Definition of term *Anaphora*

Anaphora or *Anaphoric Reference* is the process of referring back to glean meaning from something that has already been mentioned. 'The cook took off her apron. She hung it on a peg' – *her* and *she* refer back to *the cook*. *It* refers back to the apron. Anaphor is very common and perfectly normal in speech, there's nothing especially literary about it, but in the hands of an author it can be exploited to literary effect.

2 Demonstration of *Anaphora*

Here's some dialogue from a humorous novel about the doings of a London housewife:

"But seriously, Mrs. 'Opkins," I says, "you don't really mean to tell me as you made that from a pattern?"
　"Yes," she says, "I must admit as it ain't come out quite like the picture, but it ain't so bad for a beginner, is it?"
　"No-o," I says doubtful, "I suppose not. I dessay if you was to give the pattern to a blind imbycile she might make a worser job of it. I don't say she would, but she might."
　"Well," she says, "I'll lend you the pattern and you can see," which she does. She's quite a nice woman in some ways, and except for 'er face and figure, quite good-looking in 'er own style; after all, we can't all be Venices.

Clifford B. Poultney, 1923, *Mrs. 'Arris*

And here's the same dialogue, with the anaphoric reference made explicit:

"But seriously, Mrs. 'Opkins," I says, "you don't really mean to tell me as you made that (referred to previously as an 'and-knitted abortion, which had itself been referred to earlier in the text as a jumper) from a pattern?"
　"Yes," she (Mrs. 'Opkins) says, "I must admit as it (the 'and-knitted abortion) ain't come out quite like the picture, but it (the 'and-knitted abortion) ain't so bad for a beginner, is it (so bad)?"
　"No-o," I says doubtful, "I suppose not. I dessay if you was to give the pattern to a blind imbycile she (the blind imbycile) might make a worser job of it (knitting the jumper). I don't say she (the blind imbycile) would, but she (the blind imbycile) might."

"Well," she (Mrs. 'Opkins) says, "I'll lend you the pattern and you can see," which she (Mrs. 'Opkins) does. She (Mrs. 'Opkins)'s quite a nice woman in some ways, and except for 'er (Mrs. 'Opkins') face and figure, quite good-looking in 'er (Mrs. 'Opkins') own style; after all, we (women) can't all be Venices.

It would be tedious to fill in all the anaphoric references explicitly when studying a text, but our brain performs a similar exercise when we read, or when we speak and listen.

3 Literary Exercise

Below is an extract from a novel written by a Gibraltarian author in the local language, a mix of Spanish, English and other languages which is known as *Llanito*. What is it that *this story* in the antepenultimate sentence points back to?

Neither Manu nor his mum had anything to do with *el Pantera* when they came to live in Macphail's Passage, a stone's throw away from Castle Road, but it could be argued that his shadow always loomed over his son and for this reason I'm going to include a few words here about him. His real name was Johnny Rogelio and he lived in a detached house on Engineer Road, just past *el Casino*. He must have been forty-six or forty-seven when I first saw *el muy cabrón*. Paunchy but stocky dude, one of those guys who are unprepossessing from a distance, but from up close give you the creeps. He had a nose like Doña Rogelia's and a face as furrowed as a *Spitting Image* puppet. He also owned a gigantic head of grey hair that fell in greasy, yellowing locks onto his denim-jacketed shoulders – giving him the appearance, when you saw him riding through Queensway on his Harley Fat Bob, of a superannuated but sexually promiscuous rock star. Like many tough guys of his generation, he wore pointy cowboy boots and he loved nothing better than to strut up and down Main Street or Irish Town in those wooden-heeled size twelves, sowing terror and alarm just with the sound of that metronomic clickety-clack. Fellow hoodlums lowered their eyes in his presence. Grown men grew pale and crossed the road. Middle-aged women dragged their teenage daughters aside, instinctively interpolating their matronly bodies between their darlings and the eyes of the *sinvergüenza* prowling before them. He was known as '*el Pantera*' because he had a tattoo of a panther etched on his lower abdomen, the tail of which, allegedly, was painted on a long but disproportionately thin penis. In summer, when he used to sit with his *contrabandista* mates knocking back Heinekens and smoking sneaky *porros* at the Dolphin Bar in Camp Bay, getting more and more smashed as the afternoon wore on, you could see the head and shoulders of the panther snaking out of his half-unbuttoned jeans, its open jaws and tongue visible beneath a thick tangle of abdominal hair. It was one of the most ridiculous things imaginable, but it was also his personal talisman, the semi-mythical emblem that turned him into a larger-than-life figure and – rendered him into an object of sexual fascination. We all know how this story goes, don't we? *'La tiene tan larga, o no la tiene?'*[5] 'Tis a question, my dear reader, that must have tipped more than one inebriated damsel into those giant *gitano* arms.

M. G. Sanchez, *Marlboro Man*, 2021

5 'Does he really have such a long one?'

Analysis

All the *he/him/his* pronouns in this extract refer back to the character firstly referred to as *el Pantera* and subsequently as Johnny Rogelio, *el muy cabrón* ('bastard') and the *sinvergüenza* ('scoundrel'). *This story* refers back in the text to the myth reported two sentences earlier about Johnny's penis being allegedly long and thin, but it also alludes to what the sociolinguist Dirk Geeraerts has called 'stereotypical knowledge'. Stereotypicality in Geeraerts' sense is a social property: what an adult speaker of a language knows about the social meaning of a word or phrase over and above its semantic meaning. As an example, the phrase 'size matters' carries social meaning – adult speakers know that 'size matters' isn't as general as it sounds but refers specifically to penises, and they know that the social occasion on which it allegedly matters is a sexual one – plus they also know that it isn't really true. 'Size matters' carries with it a bawdy sort of humour. When reaching "We all know how this story goes, don't we?", the reader is primed for 'this story' being an anaphoric reference not only to Johnny's penis retrospectively but also to what he is going to be doing with it in pages to come.

Reference

Geeraerts, Dirk. 2008. Prototypes, stereotypes and semantic norms. In Gitte Kristiansen & René Dirven (eds.), *Cognitive Sociolinguistics: Language Variation, Cultural Models, Social Systems*, 21–44. Berlin: Mouton de Gruyter. For more on stereotype theory see Chapter 5 in Wright, Laura. 2023. *The Social Life of Words*. Oxford: Blackwells.

Commentary

M. G. Sanchez codeswitches into Llanito throughout *Marlboro Man*, sometimes translated in a footnote and sometimes not. *'La tiene tan larga, o no la tiene?'*, is translated in a footnote as 'Does he really have such a long one?' A literal translation is: 'The _ he-has so long, or not the _ he-has', where the underscore indicates an elided noun. Spanish nouns are gendered, meaning that *la* refers anaphorically to a feminine noun already mentioned. But which noun is it? The word 'penis' in Spanish is masculine, *el pene*, so it cannot be that. The panther tattoo might be a contender because in Spanish the noun 'panther' is feminine, *la pantera*, but here it is premodified by the masculine article *el* because *el Pantera* is Johnny's nickname and Johnny's biological gender is masculine. In fact *la* does indeed refer anaphorically back to Johnny's penis, but the Llanito word that Gibraltarians use is not *el pene* but *la polla* – which also means 'hen'. Germanic and Slavonic languages also share the same bird metaphor: *cock* in English, *hahn* in German, *кур* in Bulgarian (Cooper 2008, Immonen 2014).

References

Cooper, Brian. 2008. Contribution to the study of a euphemism in the intimate lexis of Slavonic and Germanic Languages. *Transactions of the Philological Society* 106(1). 71–91.

Immonen, Visa. 2014. Fondling on the kitchen table – artefacts, sexualities and performative metaphors from the 15th to the 17th centuries. *Journal of Social Archaeology* 14(2). 177–195.

4 Teaching Point

Anaphoric reference and pronouns go together, as pronouns often refer back to a previously-mentioned noun. In speech, pronouns and the pro-verb *do* are very common, more common than Proper Nouns, probably because we always speak in context. We always know what we are talking about and so don't need to repeat people's names or the names of things as we do when writing. Using fewer pronouns in subject position than in speech has become one of the conventions of written Standard English.

20 On Cataphora

1 Definition of term *Cataphora*

Cataphora or Cataphoric Reference is the process of looking forward in a text to make sense of it.

> 'Noticing that it covered the roof opposite, Reginald realised that snow had fallen overnight.'

It isn't until you reach the word *snow* that you can correctly interpret the pronoun *it*. *It* and *snow* are co-referential; they refer to the same entity. Authors can use cataphora as a delaying tactic for stylistic effect.

2 Demonstration of *Cataphora*

The following extract is taken from the beginning of a novel. I have coloured blue the co-referential elements; see if you agree with my choice.

It aint like your regular sort of day.
    Bernie pulls me a pint and puts it in front of me. He looks at me, puzzled, with his loose, doggy face but he can tell I don't want no chit-chat. That's why I'm here, five minutes after opening, for a little silent pow-wow with a pint glass. He can see the black tie, though it's four days since the funeral. I hand him a fiver and he takes it to the till and brings back my change. He puts the coins, extra gently, eyeing me, on the bar beside my pint.
    'Won't be the same, will it?' he says, shaking his head and looking a little way along the bar, like at unoccupied space. 'Won't be the same.'
    I say, 'You aint seen the last of him yet.'
    He says, 'You what?'
    I sip the froth off my beer. 'I said you aint seen the last of him yet.'
    He frowns, scratching his cheek, looking at me. 'Course, Ray,' he says and moves off down the bar.
    I never meant to make no joke of it.
    I suck an inch off my pint and light up a snout. There's maybe three or four other early-birds apart from me, and the place don't look its best. Chilly, a whiff of disinfectant, too much empty space. There's a shaft of sunlight coming through the window, full of specks. Makes you think of a church.

I sit there, watching the old clock, up behind the bar. *Thos. Slattery, Clockmaker, Southwark*. The bottles racked up like organ pipes.

Lenny's next to arrive. He's not wearing a black tie, he's not wearing a tie at all. He takes a quick shufty at what I'm wearing and we both feel we gauged it wrong.

'Let me, Lenny,' I say. 'Pint?'

He says, 'This is a turn-up.'

Bernie comes over. He says, 'New timetable, is it?'

'Morning,' Lenny says.

'Pint for Lenny,' I say.

'Retired now, have we, Lenny?' Bernie says.

'Past the age for it, aint I, Bern? I aint like Raysy here, man of leisure. Fruit and veg trade needs me.'

'But not today, eh?' Bernie says.

Bernie draws the pint and moves off to the till.

'You haven't told him?' Lenny says, looking at Bernie.

'No,' I say, looking at my beer, then at Lenny.

Lenny lifts his eyebrows. His face looks raw and flushed. It always does, like it's going to come out in a bruise. He tugs at his collar where his tie isn't.

'It's a turn-up,' he says. 'And Amy aint coming? I mean, she aint changed her mind?'

'No,' I say. 'Down to us, I reckon. The inner circle.'

'[Her own husband](),' he says.

He takes hold of his pint but he's slow to start drinking, as if there's different rules today even for drinking a pint of beer.

'We going to Vic's?' he says.

'No, Vic's coming here,' I say.

He nods, lifts his glass, then checks it, sudden, half-way to his mouth. His eyebrows go even higher.

I say, 'Vic's coming here. With [Jack](). Drink up, Lenny.'

Vic arrives about five minutes later. He's wearing a black tie but you'd expect that, seeing as he's an undertaker, seeing as he's just come from his premises. But he's not wearing his full rig. He's wearing a fawn raincoat, with a flat cap poking out of one of the pockets, as if he's aimed to pitch it right: he's just one of us, it aint official business, it's different.

'Morning,' he says.

I've been wondering what he'll have with him. So's Lenny, I dare say. Like I've had this picture of Vic opening the pub door and marching in, all solemn, with a little oak casket with brass fittings. But all he's carrying, under one arm, is a plain brown cardboard box, about a foot high and six inches square. He looks like a man who's been down the shops and bought a set of bathroom tiles.

He parks himself on the stool next to Lenny, putting the box on the bar, unbuttoning his raincoat.

'Fresh out,' he says.

'Is that it then?' Lenny says, looking. 'Is that him?'

'Yes,' Vic says. 'What are we drinking?'

'What's inside?' Lenny says.

'What do you think?' Vic says.

He twists the box round so we can see there's a white card sellotaped to one side. There's a date and a number and name: JACK ARTHUR DODDS.

Graham Swift, 1996, *Last Orders*

Note on dialect: the novel is written in London English. A *snout* is a cigarette or cigar. *This is a turn-up* implies that Raysy doesn't normally offer to buy Lenny a pint of beer, or to start the round of drinks-buying, or at least not at that time in the morning. The *full rig* refers to undertakers' professional uniform of formal black jacket, trousers, waistcoat and tie.

When you have finished reading the last three words, you realise that it is the cremated remains of Jack Arthur Dodds that are in the box. The elements which refer cataphorically to Jack Arthur Dodds are '*You aint seen the last of him yet*', '*I said you aint seen the last of him yet*', '*Her own husband*', '*Is that it then?*', '*Is that him?*'. The pronouns *him* and *it*, and the phrase *her own husband* can all be replaced by *Jack Arthur Dodds*. The pronoun *it* in *I never meant to make no joke of it* could also be replaced by *Jack Arthur Dodds* – or you may interpret *it* in this context as the business of Raysy telling Bernie that Jack Arthur Dodd's mortal remains will soon be back in the pub.

As we begin reading this novel we can't make sense of the dialogue. We have to bear with it for three pages (in the paperback version). Using cataphora can be a risky strategy: some readers may give up before the pay-off, others will find it intriguing.

3 Literary Exercise

Identify the cataphoric reference in the following extract from Virginia Woolf's novel *Mrs Dalloway*, first published in 1925. Does it make it easy to follow?

For having lived in Westminster – how many years now? over twenty, – one feels even in the midst of the traffic, or waking at night, Clarissa was positive, a particular hush, or solemnity; an indescribable pause; a suspense (but that might be her heart, affected, they said, by influenza) before Big Ben strikes. There! Out it boomed. First a warning, musical; then the hour, irrevocable. The leaden circles dissolved in the air. Such fools we are, she thought, crossing Victoria Street. For Heaven only knows why one loves it so, how one sees it so, making it up, building it round one, tumbling it, creating it every moment afresh; but the veriest frumps, the most dejected of miseries sitting on doorsteps (drink their downfall) do the same; can't be dealt with, she felt positive, by Acts of Parliament for that very reason: they love life. In people's eyes, in the swing, tramp, and trudge; in the bellow and the uproar; the carriages, motor cars, omnibuses, vans, sandwich men shuffling and swinging; brass bands; barrel organs; in the triumph and the jingle and the strange high singing of some aeroplane overhead was what she loved; life; London; this moment of June.

Virginia Woolf, 1925, *Mrs Dalloway*

Semantic note: the meaning of the word *frump* has changed slightly. The *Oxford English Dictionary* defines *frump*, n. 5. a. as a 'cross, old-fashioned, dowdily-dressed woman', and this meaning still pertains, but alcoholic women who live on the streets are no longer described as frumps. Today the word *frump* pertains to a woman who has a dowdy appearance; to be a *frump* is to be without allure.

Analysis

Here is the text with the cataphoric reference made explicit. As with anaphoric reference, there can be more than one referent and you may have different interpretations.

For having lived in Westminster – how many years now? over twenty, – one feels even in the midst of the traffic, or waking at night, Clarissa was positive, a particular hush, or solemnity; an indescribable pause; a suspense (but that might be her heart, affected, they said, by influenza) before Big Ben strikes. There! Out it boomed. First a warning, musical; then the hour, irrevocable. The leaden circles dissolved in the air. Such fools we are, she thought, crossing Victoria Street. For Heaven only knows why one loves it (life/London/this moment of June) so, how one sees it (life/London/this moment of June) so, making it (life) up, building it (life/this moment of June) round one, tumbling it (life), creating it (life) every moment afresh; but the veriest frumps, the most dejected of miseries sitting on doorsteps (drink their downfall) do (love life) the same; can't be dealt with, she felt positive, by Acts of Parliament for that very reason: they love life. In people's eyes, in the swing, tramp, and trudge; in the bellow and the uproar; the carriages, motor cars, omnibuses, vans, sandwich men shuffling and swinging; brass bands; barrel organs; in the triumph and the jingle and the strange high singing of some aeroplane overhead was what she loved; life; London; this moment of June.

Commentary

This extract is taken from the second page of the novel. At this point, Clarissa is setting off from her home in Westminster, crossing Victoria Street and observing what she hears and sees. This paragraph is about her present. Notice how the pronoun *it* in the seventh sentence could refer, anaphorically, to Victoria Street – ("For Heaven only knows why one loves it (Victoria Street) so, how one sees it (Victoria Street) so, making it (Victoria Street) up, building it (Victoria Street) round one, tumbling it (Victoria Street), creating it (Victoria Street) every moment afresh") but this interpretation does not work well semantically: one can't tumble Victoria Street, or create Victoria Street, or build Victoria Street round one. However this only becomes apparent as we read on. At the beginning of the sequence: "Such fools we are, she thought, crossing Victoria Street. For Heaven only knows why one loves it so, how one sees it so," – anaphoric reference is perfectly plausible. It's only as we continue in the sentence that we realise we have to rule it out and look forwards in the text instead of backwards. I have put *life/London/this moment of June* as the cataphoric referent of the pronoun *it*, but I don't know whether Virginia Woolf meant them as synonyms, or as a hierarchically-ordered sequence, where *life* comes before *London*, which comes before *this moment in June*. Are the three collapsed into one 'present' for Clarissa, or does *life* trump *London* and *this June moment*?

It's actually quite hard to write, in a sustained way, about the present, the present moment being rather intangible. As we read this passage we have to suspend our understanding for a short while. We too have to experience a pause, momentarily, before we understand that Big Ben strikes, and we have to bear with Clarissa – again, momentarily – as she reflects upon making it up, building it round, tumbling it and creating it, before we finally arrive at knowing what 'it' is: loving living here and now.

This passage is poignant, as Virginia Woolf took her own life. Living, loving life, having a present, was also a precarious business for the specific subset of people she mentions, "the veriest frumps, the most dejected of miseries sitting on doorsteps (drink their downfall)". The Eugenics Education Society, created in 1906, met at Denison House in Victoria Street. Its purpose was 'to promote the mental, moral and physical improvement of the race', and during Virginia's lifetime this society was concerned with women alcoholics, because it was thought that if women were alcoholics "young England would be drunk before it was born" (*The Times* 28/02/1908). In 1908 the Inebriate Homes, which cared for six hundred women, had been closed in a quarrel over who paid the costs. The Government decided it should henceforth be the responsibility of the London County Council, so the London County Council provided space for a hundred of the inebriate women who were likely to reform, and cast the other five hundred back onto the streets because they were deemed incorrigible. This was known as returning them to the "Jane Cakebread condition". Jane Cakebread was an alcoholic Londoner who repeatedly came before the courts for being drunk and disorderly – she had 282 convictions by 1893. Another alcoholic called Ellen Sweeney had 279 convictions by 1895, and they were not alone. The Inebriates Act of 1898 was passed in order to treat alcoholics, rather than to repeatedly lock them up as criminals, but the costs impacted too greatly on the London County Council and so the homes were closed and the women went back on the streets. In 1910 the Women's Total Abstinence Union also met at Denison House and announced that in one school alone 40% of the children drank alcohol regularly. Loving life, in the context of the frumps and miseries of Victoria Street, was not the carefree concept it may sound.

4 Teaching Point

Cataphoric reference always has a delaying effect of some sort. It's not a particularly unusual linguistic feature, and it's even a staple of newspaper headlines. *Get off your mobile or I won't serve you* reads tonight's headline, causing viewers to read further in the paper to find out who *I* refers to.

21 End Focus and Endweight

1 Definition of term *End Focus and Endweight*

Endweight refers to the observation that "complex or 'heavy' sentence constituents will tend to follow simpler or lighter ones" (Wales 2000: 145). When variation is possible, endweight explains the choice of ordering. Consider the following examples: in the 1960s, dresses were fastened up the back with long zips. A mother might use the verb to fasten in its *imperative* (command) form to her child:
a) Fasten the zip on your long black dress.
b) On your long black dress, fasten the zip.
c) Fasten – on your long black dress – the zip.

a) observes the endweight principle. b) and c) are stylistically marked for specific effect. Although the outcome will be the same in all three cases and the dress will be fastened, they don't mean exactly the same thing: b) implies that there is another zip to be attended to ("on your long black dress fasten the zip but leave your anorak undone") or that further instructions about getting ready are to follow, and c) might be said if the child reaches for another garment. a) is known as *canonical ordering*, and is the unmarked choice. It can be described as (S) V X, where the Subject (*you*) in this case is elided, the finite verb, an imperative, is *fasten*, and everything else is labelled X. SVX is canonical ordering in English. Examples b) and c) shift the emphasis on to some other part of the sentence. This shifting of emphasis can be very useful for authors wishing to give nuances of meaning.

The endweight principle leads to another principle, that of *end focus*:

> *End focus* "is based on the general fact that different parts of utterances have different communicative values . . . and that normally NEW or important INFORMATION is reserved for the end." (Wales 2000: 126)

The implication here is that old information, stuff we already know, is likely to come in the Subject, and can be quickly dealt with by reducing it to a pronoun or eliding it altogether; and new information is likely to come in the X constituents. Being new, it is likely to receive a fuller treatment.

Reference

Wales, Katie. 2000 [1989]. *A Dictionary of Stylistics*. Harlow: Longman, pp 144–5.

2 Demonstration of *End focus and Endweight*

Read through this description of a London suburb, bearing in mind the principles of endweight and end focus.

In the straight streets planted with trees and fringed with grass plots stand the modern houses where the families live. These houses have quite different sorts of names from the old houses. The modern names are written on the garden gates or slung in fretwork over the porch. The Cedars, Cumfy, Dunromin, the more original Dunsekin, Trottalong. There is the house that is called Home Rails (a happy investment, fortune-founding?). There is Deo Data for the learned, Villa Roma for the travelled, Portarlington Lodge for the socially ambitious. Ella, Basil and Ronald live at Elbasron. There is also Elasofton which is 'not for sale' written backwards.

    The place names on the way to the city where the fathers go daily to earn their living are countrified – the mysterious Cockfosters, Green Lanes, Wood Green, Turnpike Lane. Coming nearer to the city there is Manor Park. And what is that curious building, an exact copy of Stirling Castle, that stands to the left of the bus route? It is the Waterworks.

Stevie Smith, 1949, *A London Suburb*

Here is the text again. I have marked the X elements in light blue, the V elements in mauve, and the S elements in red.

[In the straight streets planted with trees and fringed with grass plots]X [stand]V [the modern houses where the families live.]S [These houses]S [have]V [quite different sorts of names from the old houses.]X [The modern names]S [are written]V [on the garden gates or slung in fretwork over the porch.]X [The Cedars, Cumfy, Dunromin, the more original Dunsekin, Trottalong.]S [There]S [is]V [the house that is called Home Rails (a happy investment, fortune-founding?)]X [There]S [is]V [Deo Data for the learned, Villa Roma for the travelled, Portarlington Lodge for the socially ambitious.]X [Ella, Basil and Ronald]S [live]V [at Elbasron.]X [There]S [is]V [also Elasofton which is 'not for sale' written backwards.]X

    [The place names on the way to the city where the fathers go daily to earn their living]S [are]V [countrified – the mysterious Cockfosters, Green Lanes, Wood Green, Turnpike Lane.]X [Coming nearer to the city]X [there]S [is]V [Manor Park.]X [And]X [what]S [is]V [that curious building, an exact copy of Stirling Castle, that stands to the left of the bus route?]X [It]S [is]V [the Waterworks.]X

The first sentence is not SVX but XVS – try changing it around to get canonical ordering: *the modern houses where the families live stand in the straight streets planted with trees and fringed with grass plots*. What does Stevie Smith's ordering achieve that canonical ordering does not? Endweight throws the emphasis onto the S, *the modern houses where the families live*, in particular, the *families* – try saying it aloud. The passage is about the family house of the outer suburbs as opposed to the London townhouse – Stevie Smith wrote this in 1949, when the immense spread of semi-detached housing that created the outer suburbs between the two world wars was relatively new. She spent almost her entire life in such a house in such a suburb at 1, Avondale Road, Palmers Green, N13.

End focus is the principle of given to new information, and in the first sentence the modern houses are new information. In sentence two, the modern houses have turned into given information – *these houses*, and hereafter the endweight principle is observed. The end focus of the X is *the old houses*, bringing them into contrast with the modern ones, and the new information is the houses' names. In sentence three, the modern houses and their names have become given information: *The modern names* (the fourth sentence lacks a finite verb and so is not actually a sentence but a list of names). Thereafter come the various names, introduced four times by *There is*. In the constructions *there is* and *it is*, the Subjects *there* and *it* are referred to as 'dummy subjects' when they lack an obvious referent. In such cases *there* and *it* lacks semantic meaning and act as grammatical placeholders. Compare *There is the house that is called Home Rails, There is Deo Data, There is also Elasofton*, where *there* lacks any semantic meaning, with *It is the Waterworks*, where *it* refers back to the building that looks like Stirling Castle and hence is not a dummy subject but a pronoun standing in for *the castle*. (Compare *It is raining* to see *it* acting as a dummy subject.) *There* and *It* are very light Subjects; the heavy constituents mostly come after the Verb and are where the new information is elaborated. The poet appreciates the suburban house-names, the puns, the disguised waterworks – all ways of deflating pomp with a joke.

Note: what were *Home Rails*? "Her own fortune was invested in Home Rails, and most ardently did she beg her niece to imitate her." (E. M. Forster, *Howards End*, 1910); "Home Rails, which are now in effect British Transport stock" (*Railway Gazette International*, 1947).

3 Literary Exercise

Read through the following poem, bearing the principles of end focus and endweight in mind. Although you are expecting to see end focus and endweight, along with canonical SVX ordering, writers flout these principles for effect. What happens here?

On the Dressing gown lent me by my Hostess the Brazilian Consul in Milan, 1958

1. Dear Daughter of the Southern Cross
2. I admit your fiery nature and your loss

3. Your fiery integrity and your intelligence
4. I admit your high post and its relevance

5. And I admit, dear Consuelessa, that your dressing gown
6. Has wrapped me from the offences of the town.

7. From rain in Milan in a peculiar May
8. From anger at break of day
9. From heat and cold as I lay

10. Wrapped me, but not entirely, from the words I must hear
11. Thrown between you and him, that were not 'dear'.

12. Oh that him
13. Was a problem
14. Consuelessa, your husband.

15. He and I ran together in the streets, I think
16. We grew more English with each drink
17. And we laughed as we ran in the town
18. Consuelessa, where then was your dressing gown?

19. The Portuguese and the Italian languages
20. Drew our laughter in stages
21. Of infantine rages,
22. This was outrageous.

23. Yes, I admit your courage, I heard
24. Heart steel at the word
25. That found everything absurd,
26. The English word I spoke and heard.

27. Tapping at your heels, Consuelessa,
28. We were children again, your husband and I,
29. A worthless couple,

30. Hanging behind, whining, being slow,
31. 'Where is our wife?' we cry. (This you knew.)
32. 'Give us money' we said, 'you have not given us much'.
33. We were your kiddies, Consuelessa, out for a touch.

34. Yet I admit your dressing gown
35. Wrapped me from the offences of the town
36. But never from my own
37. Ah Consuelessa, this much I own.

38. From rain in May
39. From the cold as I lay
40. When the servant Cesare had stolen
41. The electric fire, the only one,
42. From disappointment too I daresay
43. Consuelessa,
44. It is your dressing gown I remember today.

Stevie Smith, first published 1981, *On the Dressing gown lent me by my Hostess the Brazilian Consul in Milan, 1958*

Here is the poem again. I have marked the X elements in light blue, the V elements in mauve, and the S elements in red.

1. Dear Daughter of the Southern Cross
2. I admit your fiery nature and your loss

3. Your fiery integrity and your intelligence
4. I admit your high post and its relevance

5. And I admit, dear Consuelessa, that your dressing gown
6. Has wrapped me from the offences of the town.

7. From rain in Milan in a peculiar May
8. From anger at break of day
9. From heat and cold as I lay

10. Wrapped me, but not entirely, from the words I must hear
11. Thrown between you and him, that were not 'dear'.

12. Oh that him
13. Was a problem
14. Consuelessa, your husband.

15. He and I ran together in the streets, I think
16. We grew more English with each drink
17. And we laughed as we ran in the town

18. Consuelessa, where then was your dressing gown?
19. The Portuguese and the Italian languages
20. Drew our laughter in stages
21. Of infantine rages,
22. This was outrageous.
23. Yes, I admit your courage, I heard
24. Heart steel at the word
25. That found everything absurd,
26. The English word I spoke and heard.
27. Tapping at your heels, Consuelessa,
28. We were children again, your husband and I,
29. A worthless couple,
30. Hanging behind, whining, being slow,
31. 'Where is our wife?' we cry. (This you knew.)
32. 'Give us money' we said, 'you have not given us much'.
33. We were your kiddies, Consuelessa, out for a touch.
34. Yet I admit your dressing gown
35. Wrapped me from the offences of the town
36. But never from my own
37. Ah Consuelessa, this much I own.
38. From rain in May
39. From the cold as I lay
40. When the servant Cesare had stolen
41. The electric fire, the only one,
42. From disappointment too I daresay
43. Consuelessa,
44. It is your dressing gown I remember today.

Analysis

The Subjects are mainly light, with the exception of lines 12 and 14, where the subject has two synonyms (*that him* and *your husband*). Occurring where it does in the middle of the poem, this three-liner forms a crux. Endweight puts the emphasis onto *your husband*. At lines 28 and 29 the heavier Subjects (*your husband and I, a worthless couple*) are synonymous with *we*. The Verb Phrases are light, but the verb *admit* is repeated five times, and its synonym *own* once. Canonical ordering is relatively as expected apart from the last stanza. Here the X element is mainly fronted, and the reader or listener has to refer back to lines 5–9 to work out that the narrator is reflecting on how the Consuelessa's dressing gown wrapped her from the various adversities detailed in the series of Prepositional Phrases and clauses in lines 38–42. In line 44, endweight puts emphasis on *I remember today*.

Commentary

The poem is a letter from the narrator to the Brazilian Consul, who, at some point in the relatively recent past, was a married lady with a grievance. It transpires that the narrator gave offence by fooling around with the Consuelessa's husband – not explicitly sexually, but enough to cause jealousy: she laughed complicitly, spoke English, mocked and got drunk with him to the exclusion of the Consuelessa, causing an early morning argument between husband and wife. The narrator, reflecting upon the kindness of the borrowed dressing gown, admits guilt. The narrator's conscience causes her to remember with clarity her individual offences against the Consuelessa, as opposed to the Consuelessa's kindness to her. Remorse is implicit in the list of admissions.

What is the loss mentioned in line 2? Did the Consuelessa lose her husband as a result?

4 Teaching Point

In English, the principles of end focus and endweight work together to create a canonical ordering of SVX, where S is typically light (one-word, elided or dummy subjects, pronouns) and X is heavy. However, writers can disturb this order to shift emphasis.

22 Collocation and Colligation

1 Definition of term collocation and colligation

The term collocation refers to the company words keep. *Bacon* collocates with *eggs*. *Rancid* collocates with *butter*. *Health* collocates with *and safety*. In public announcements, *apologies* collocates with *for any inconvenience caused*. Collocations can be in any relation – within the phrase, clause, or above clause level. They can stay stable for centuries: *aid* goes with *and abet*, and has done since Anglo-Norman French was the language of the law. They can also shift rapidly: people didn't call each other a *silly juggins* before the mid 1800s and they haven't done so for several decades. But the collocation *silly juggins* occurs in novels by Sir Arthur Conan Doyle (*The Three Correspondents*, 1896), Jerome K. Jerome (*Paul Kelver*, 1902), Compton Mackenzie (*The Early Life and Adventures of Sylvia Scarlet*, 1918), Agatha Christie (*The Seven Dials Mystery*, 1929) and others of that generation. If you go to the Google Ngram Viewer at http://books.google.com/ngrams and type in "silly juggins" you'll see a heyday of usage in the decade 1910–1920, with a flanking of vanguard and rearguard users, and what is probably restricted usage from the 1940s onwards – restricted to literature written for children, or in more recent decades, ironic use.

Colligation is a type of collocation where a lexical item is tied to a grammatical one. *It's not the end of the world* is a common locution, however, its synonym *it's not Armageddon* is not. The phrase *the end of the world* colligates with the negative, whereas *Armageddon* doesn't. Collocation and colligation are therefore useful ways of looking at synonyms: words may mean the same thing, but turn out to keep different company.

2 Demonstration of term *collocation and colligation* in action

Read the beginning of Chapter Three from *Where Angels Fear to Tread* by E. M. Forster, and consider whether there are any unusual collocations or colligations:

Opposite the Volterra gate of Monteriano, outside the city, is a very respectable white-washed mud wall, with a coping of red crinkled tiles to keep it from dissolution. It would suggest a gentleman's garden if there was not in its middle a large hole, which grows larger with every rain-storm. Through the hole is visible, firstly, the iron gate that is intended to close it; secondly, a square piece of ground which, though not quite, mud, is at the same time not exactly grass; and finally, another wall, stone this time, which has a wooden door in the middle and two wooden-shuttered windows each side, and apparently forms the façade of a one-storey house.

This house is bigger than it looks, for it slides for two storeys down the hill behind, and the wooden door, which is always locked, really leads into the attic. The knowing person prefers to follow the precipitous mule-track round the turn of the mud wall till he can take the edifice in the rear. Then—being now on a level with the cellars—he lifts up his head and shouts. If his voice sounds like something light—a letter, for example, or some vegetables, or a bunch of flowers—a basket is let out of the first-floor windows by a string, into which he puts his burdens and departs. But if he sounds like something heavy, such as a log of wood, or a piece of meat, or a visitor, he is interrogated, and then bidden or forbidden to ascend. The ground floor and the upper floor of that battered house are alike deserted, and the inmates keep the central portion, just as in a dying body all life retires to the heart. There is a door at the top of the first flight of stairs, and if the visitor is admitted he will find a welcome which is not necessarily cold. There are several rooms, some dark and mostly stuffy—a reception-room adorned with horsehair chairs, wool-work stools, and a stove that is never lit—German bad taste without German domesticity broods over that room; also a living-room, which insensibly glides into a bedroom when the refining influence of hospitality is absent, and real bedrooms; and last, but not least, the loggia, where you can live day and night if you feel inclined, drinking vermouth and smoking cigarettes, with leagues of olive-trees and vineyards and blue-green hills to watch you.

E. M. Forster, 1905, *Where Angels Fear to Tread*

The Noun Phrase *a very respectable white-washed mud wall* contains a head noun, *wall*, premodified by two adjectives, *white-washed* and *mud*, and two adverbs, *very* and *respectable*. The internal constituents of the Adverbial Phrase [*very respectable*] and the Noun Phrase [*white-washed mud wall*] collocate with each other, but the Adverbial Phrase does not usually collocate with the Noun Phrase. [*very respectable*] usually collocates either with humans, or with entities grander than a mud wall, such as *Oxford English Dictionary* respectable, adj. and n. A. adj. 3. b. "The fourth floor more resembled the inside of a drinkers' den than a respectable place of business."

This house is bigger than it looks, for it slides for two storeys down the hill behind: the noun *house* does not usually collocate with the verb *slide*, unless talking about an earthquake. It suggests movement, and animates the house, as does *a living-room, which insensibly glides into a bedroom*, where the noun *living-room* does not usually collocate with the verb *glides*. By contrast, the noun *door* (*the wooden door, which is always locked, really leads into the attic*) does collocate with the verb *lead* and so can't be said to particularly lend animation.

If his voice sounds like something light; if he sounds like something heavy: the adjectives *light* and *heavy* do not usually collocate with the verb *sound*, and this is a snappy way of conveying the household customs.

bidden or forbidden: despite their obvious relationship, these two verbs do not usually collocate together.

a welcome which is not necessarily cold: the collocation *a warm welcome* lies behind this periphrasis [*periphrasis*: a circumlocution, using several words where few would do].

The overall effect of these mild surprises is one of equally mild humour. The description of the house is not out-and-out funny but there is a lightness of touch here, a sprightliness – and this style characterizes much of E. M. Forster's writing.

3 Literary Exercise

Read the following passage and comment on the effect of any interesting or unusual collocations. The footnote is in the original text.

Miss Mouse (in a very enterprising frock by Cheruit) sat on a chair with her eyes popping out of her head. She never *could* get used to so much excitement, never. Tonight she had brought a little friend with her – a Miss Brown – because it was so much more fun if one had someone to talk to. It was too thrilling to see all that dull money her father had amassed, metamorphosed in this way into so much glitter and noise and so many bored young faces. Archie Schwert, as he passed, champagne bottle in hand, paused to say, "How are you, Mary darling? Quite all right?"

"That's Archie Schwert," said Miss Mouse to Miss Brown. "Isn't he too clever?"

"Is he?" said Miss Brown, who would have liked a drink, but didn't know how quite to set about it. "You *are* lucky to know such amusing people, Mary darling. I never see anyone."

"Wasn't the invitation clever? Johnnie Hoop wrote it."

"Well, yes, I suppose it was. But you know (was it dreadful of me?) I hadn't heard of any of the names."*

* Perhaps it should be explained – there were at this time three sorts of formal invitation card; there was the nice sensible copybook hand sort with a name and *At Home* and a date and time and address; then there was the sort that came from Chelsea, *Noel and Audrey are having a little whoopee on Saturday evening: do please come and bring a bottle too, if you can*; and finally there was the sort that Johnnie Hoop used to adapt from *Blast* and Marinetti's *Futurist Manifesto*. These had two columns of close print; in one was a list of all the things Johnnie hated, and in

the other all the things he thought he liked. Most of the parties which Miss Mouse financed had invitations written by Johnnie Hoop.

Evelyn Waugh, 1930, *Vile Bodies*

Analysis

You may have noticed the Noun Phrase *a very enterprising frock*, as the adjective *enterprising* does not usually modify the noun *frock*, but the collocates that are unlikely to be in your own idiolect are *too thrilling* and *having a little whoopee on Saturday evening*.

The adverb *too*, used as an intensifier, is found in the *Oxford English Dictionary* under too, *adv.* II. 3. As a mere intensive: Excessively, extremely, exceedingly, very. ('Now chiefly an emotional feminine colloquialism') — this observation dates from 1913 and is probably the opinion of the lexicographer rather than based on any survey, but it shows that *too* as an intensifier was perceived as being used by some speakers and not by others at that date. Mary Mouse's pronouncement about Archie Schwert's being too clever is in response to his perfectly normal greeting *How are you, Mary darling? Quite all right?* Elsewhere in the novel a character uses the double form *too, too sick-making*.

Whoopee is used as a synonym for 'party', as in the collocation 'we're having a little party'. This seems to have had a limited use in space and time. The *Oxford English Dictionary* under headword whoopee, *int. and n.*, lists one other token (with verb *give* rather than *have*):

> 1929 *Punch* 24 July 86/2 A London hostess , writing to a gossip page, said—'I am giving a Whoopee. Do come to it.'

A search of Google Books (books.google.co.uk) reveals [*having + a whoopee*] as an adjective at this date, but not as a noun: *you were out having a whoopee time* (John Held, 1930); *a school of frogs or turtles was having a whoopee party* (*The Cavalry Journal* 25, Royal United Service Institution, 1935). The usual verb collocating with *whoopee* as a noun was not *having* but *making*, colligating without the indefinite article:

> *Another bride, another June, Another sunny honeymoon, Another season, another reason for making whoopee!* (song lyric, G. Kahn, 1928)

Go to http://books.google.com/ngrams and play around with graphs for *making whoopee, make whoopee, have a whoopee, having a whoopee, give a whoopee, at a whoopee* and other configurations.

Commentary

I conclude that either using *whoopee* as a synonym for *party* in the lexical configurations with which *party* collocated was restricted to the upper-classes in London around 1930 and hence doesn't show up in literature; or, that Noel and Audrey were meant to sound inept; or, that Waugh got his slang wrong. Personally, I'm inclined to trust the author, and interpret this as a little dig at people from Chelsea, as the novel is full of little digs at people of various social types.

4 Teaching Point

Learning which words collocate with which and colligate with which is one of the demands of learning a second language, as native speakers don't get them wrong. However, inventing new collocations, or colligating them in new ways, is one of the prerogatives of creative writers, and they will always startle, to a greater or lesser extent.

23 Cohesion and Coherence

1 Definition of terms *Cohesion* and *Coherence*

Cohesion refers to the many ways (grammatical, lexical, semantic, metrical, alliterative) in which the elements of a text are linked together. *Cohesion* differs from *coherence* in that a text can be internally cohesive but be incoherent – that is, make no sense. Here is a text that is grammatically and lexically cohesive, but not very coherent:

> An octopus is an air-filled curtain with seven heads and three spike-filled fingers, which poke in frills and furls at ribbon-strewed buttons.

Grammatical cohesion:

The clause-structure obeys normal English grammatical rules (the finite verb is marked in a darker colour):

[[An octopus]Noun Phrase [is] Verb Phrase [an air-filled curtain]Noun Phrase [with seven heads] and [three spike-filled fingers]Prepositional Phrases]Main Clause

[[which]Subordinator [poke]Verb Phrase [in frills and furls] [at ribbon-strewed buttons]Prepositional Phrases]Subordinate Clause

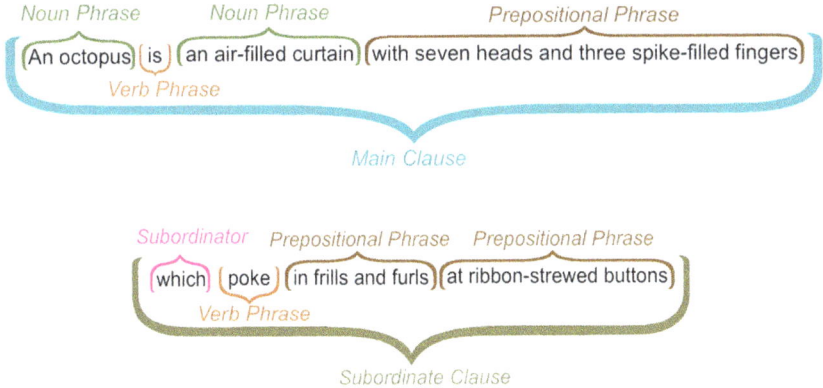

Anaphoric reference:

> *which poke* refers back to *fingers*

Lexical cohesion – semantic fields:

heads, fingers (body parts)
curtain, frills, furls, ribbons, buttons (haberdashery)

However the text only makes sense if we invent some kind of other-world context. Notice how our tendency is to want to make sense of it, to find some kind of science-fictional or poetical circumstance in which it does make sense.

Coherence

By contrast, texts can be coherent when not cohesive:

Speaker 1: Chocolate biscuits!

Speaker 2: Me! Me!

Speaker 3: Uh uh. Lent.

Readers who know that people give up things like chocolate for Lent can infer that Speaker 3 is refusing the biscuit on offer whilst Speaker 2 is enthusiastically asking for one. But nothing grammatical or lexical groups *chocolate biscuits* with *me* with *Lent*, rather it is the reader's real-world (or *exophoric*) knowledge that enables interpretation.

Cohesion is objectively identifiable; *coherence* is far more subjective, depending on the reader/listener's interpretation.

2 Demonstration of *Cohesion*

Consider the cohesion and coherence in the following dialogue:

1   'I'm thinking of getting married,' Matthew said.
2   'Oh, are you? Who to?'
3   'I haven't anyone in mind,' Matthew said. 'Only my brother-in-law thinks I should get married. My sister wants me to get married and so does my uncle. Every time I go home to Ireland my mother's ashamed that I'm not married to a girl.'
4   'I got a young woman into trouble at the age of eighteen,' Walter said. 'Daughter of one of our footmen. He was an Irish fellow. The butler caught him reading Nietzsche in the pantry. To the detriment of the silver. Of course there was no

question of my marrying his daughter. The family made a settlement and I went abroad to paint. My hair turned white at the age of nineteen.'

5   Matthew said, 'I know a girl who's expecting a baby by an old spiritualist. She's lovely. She's got long black hair.' He saddened into silence and gazed upon the girl in jeans dispassionately, recognizing her as Ronald's former girl-friend.

6   'I went abroad to paint, but my cousin the Marquise –'

7   'I'll tell you this much,' Matthew said, 'there's no justification for being a bachelor and that's the truth, let's face it. It's everyone's duty to be fruitful and multiply according to his calling either spiritual or temporal, as the case may be.'

8   'Monet admired my work. Just before he died he visited my studio with his friends, and –'

9   'These are the figures,' Matthew said, and took from inside his coat a bundle of papers from which he selected one which had been folded in four, and which was split and grubby at the folds. He straightened out the sheet, following the typewritten lines with his finger, as he read out, 'Greater London, the census of 1951. Unmarried males of twenty-one and over: six hundred and fifty-nine thousand five hundred. That's including divorced and widowed, of course, but the majority are bachelors –'

10 'I can see him now,' said Walter, 'as he was when he was assisted into a chair before my easel. Monet was silent for fully ten minutes – the painting was a simple, but rather exquisite roof-top scene –'

11 'Unmarried males of thirty and over,' said Matthew: 'three hundred and fifty-eight thousand one hundred. Since 1951 the bachelor population has increased by –'

12 'Put that vulgar little bit of paper away,' Walter said.

Muriel Spark, 1960, *The Bachelors*

Matthew begins with an observation about *marriage*. Walter answers anaphorically in paragraph 2. In paragraph 3 Matthew continues the cohesion by repeating the lexeme *marriage*. In paragraph 4, Walter uses the euphemism *got a young woman into trouble* for 'got pregnant', which is in the same semantic field as *marriage* (in the wider context of the novel, it will transpire that Walter is a fantasist), and goes on to link this to the lexeme *paint*. Matthew provides cohesion with marriage with *expecting a baby* in paragraph 5. In paragraph 6 Matthew and Walter begin to diverge: Walter continues with the lexeme *paint*. In paragraph 7 Matthew continues with pregnancy in *be fruitful and multiply*. In paragraph 8, Walter is cohesive with paragraphs 4 and 6 with the words *Monet* and *studio*. In paragraph 9, Matthew is cohesive with paragraphs 1, 2, 3, 4, 5, 7, with the lexemes *unmarried, divorced, widowed, bachelors*. In paragraph 10 Walter ignores this and continues with his own cohesion with paragraphs 4, 6, and 8 with the lexemes *him* (referring anaphorically to Monet), *easel, Monet, painting, scene*. In paragraph 11, Matthew continues with lexemes *unmarried, bachelor*, and in paragraph 12 Walter finally returns to Matthew with the word *paper*, referring anaphorically back to the *census* of paragraph 9. At no point does Matthew enter into Walter's reverie about having been an aristocratic painter. There are some more local lexical cohesions: the repetition of *hair* in paragraphs 4 and 5; *footmen, butler, pantry, silver, Marquise* in 4 and 6; the number sequences in paragraphs 9 and 11.

Both Matthew and Walter are preoccupied with their own concerns and only half pay attention to the other. Their individual texts are cohesive, but their joint discourse in the sequence paragraphs 6–11 is not. These characters are interacting, but not fully.

3 Literary Exercise

The following dialogue is extracted from Caryl Churchill's play *Top Girls*.[3] Churchill uses the following notation system:
- when one character starts speaking before the other has finished, the point of interruption is marked /
- when a speech follows on from a speech earlier than the one immediately before it, continuity is marked *

Is the dialogue cohesive, or do you think are there passages where it is not?

[They laugh. They look at menus.]

1 ISABELLA Yes, I forgot all my Latin. But my father was the mainspring of my life and when he died I was so grieved. I'll have the chicken, please, / and the soup.

2 NIJO Of course you were grieved. My father was saying his prayers and he dozed off in the sun. So I touched his knee to rouse him. 'I wonder what will happen,' he said, and then he was dead before he finished the sentence. / If he'd died saying

3 MARLENE What a shock.

---

3 © Churchill, Caryl. 1982. *Churchill Plays: Two*. London: Methuen, Drama, an imprint of Bloomsbury Publishing Plc.

4 NIJO his prayers he would have gone straight to heaven. / Waldorf salad.

5 JOAN Death is the return of all creatures to God.

6 NIJO I shouldn't have woken him.

7 JOAN Damnation only means ignorance of the truth. I was always attracted by the teachings of John the Scot, though he was inclined to confuse / God and the world.

8 ISABELLA Grief always overwhelmed me at the time.

9 MARLENE What I fancy is a rare steak. Gret?

10 ISABELLA I am of course a member of the / Church of England*

11 GRET Potatoes.

12 MARLENE *I haven't been to church for years. / I like Christmas carols.

13 ISABELLA Good works matter more than church attendance.

14 MARLENE Make that two steaks and a lot of potatoes. Rare. But I don't do good works either.

15 JOAN Canelloni, please, / and a salad.

16 ISABELLA Well, I tried, but oh dear. Hennie did good works.

17 NIJO The first half of my life was all sin and the second / all repentance*

18 MARLENE Oh what about starters?

19 GRET Soup.

20 JOAN *And which did you like best?

21 MARLENE Were your travels just a penance? Avocado vinaigrette. Didn't you / enjoy yourself?

22 JOAN Nothing to start with for me, thank you.

23 NIJO Yes, but I was very unhappy. / It hurt to remember

24 MARLENE And the wine list.

25 NIJO the past. I think that was repentance.

Caryl Churchill, 1982, *Top Girls*

Analysis

It is relatively easy, in this extract, to pick out the lexical cohesion – and the author has helped by making it explicit via her notation system. Two discourses run parallel, one about the ordering of a meal, and one about death, religion and sin. The characters Isabella, Nijo, Joan and Marlene all talk cohesively about these subjects but they almost always use the pronouns *I/me*. Gret only participates in the ordering of the meal. In particular, there are local cohesions at:

lines 1, 2, 5, 8: *grieved, grief, dead, died, death*

lines 2 and 3: *he was dead before he finished the sentence* and the anaphoric *What a shock* (that he was dead before he finished the sentence)

lines 7, 10, 12: *God, Church of England, Christmas carols*

lines 12, 13: *haven't been to church, church attendance*

lines 13, 14, 16: *good works,* and the anaphoric *I tried* (to do good works)

lines 17, 21, 25: *sin, penance, repentance*

There are other types of cohesion. There is the British politeness convention when ordering a meal, with its pleases and thankyous ("I'll have the chicken, please", "Canelloni, please", "Nothing to start with for me, thank you"). There are discourse markers [*discourse markers*, usually words or short phrases, are linking devices which indicate the speaker's attitude or shift topic]: "*Of course* you were grieved.", "*Well*, I tried, but oh dear.", "*Oh* what about starters?", "*And* which did you like best?"

Commentary

Cohesion is identifiable but it is less easy to determine the effect, especially as more than one simultaneous dialogue makes interpretation demanding for the audience, as they are bound to miss some of the dialogue. Do we regard Joan's preoccupation with God and sin as a social deficiency (she does not offer sympathy to the bereaved Isabella and Nijo), or as evidence of her religious character, or both? Are the overlaps a sign of an exuberant group of people anticipating the ends of each others' turns and enthusiastically leaping in with their own contribution, or are they indicative of inattention and social isolation? Ivanchenko (2007) points out that there is no interruption here, the discourse does not become hostile, it remains cohesive with no disjuncts, and so a relatively harmonious interpretation of joint collaboration seems preferable – but some directors have read hostility into the lines at this point.

Reference

Ivanchenko, Andriy. 2007. An 'interactive' approach to interpreting overlapping dialogue in Caryl Churchill's *Top Girls* (Act 1). *Language and Literature* 2007 16(1). 74–89.

4 Teaching Point

Dialogue is a staple of literature, but it is unlike real speech and has evolved stage conventions of its own, including discrete turn-taking. There need not be cohesion (although there usually is), but the audience has to be able to interpret the dialogue coherently.

24 Deixis

1 Definition of term *deixis*

Deictic expressions invite participants to work out connections. Deictic items point to entities in the situation in which the utterance is produced. As such, deixis is reliant on context, and shifts its referent accordingly. If I go into the café on the corner and say "One of those, please", the server and I both know what I mean, but no-one outside this context (e.g. reading a report) does. The demonstrative *those* relies entirely on the relationship between me and what is on the counter or in the cabinet, and I facilitate the server's interpretation by pointing or gaze direction. Others, reading a transcript of what was said, do not have access to the 'deictic centre', the immediate present of the person doing the speaking – which in this example is me, ordering a bun. It follows that deictic expressions shift according to who speaks: "A coffee please" from me, followed by a reply: "Is that enough?" from the server, is from the server's perspective, reliant on the relationship between the server and the milk s/he is pouring. *Enough* is deictic and will shift its meaning from context to context. In this case, I will point, or say *enough* when enough is reached.

Deixis can be of time (*then, now, when, soon, yesterday, next year*), place (*here, this, that, those over there, come, go*) and, less frequently, quantity (*enough, more, all*). The time is now 08.49.59. And now, it is 08.50.01. The sun is shining here (where I am sitting) but not here (where I have moved to). Social relationships can also be expressed deictically: *Some wine, Sir?* versus *Alf! Come and get it!* express different relationships to the speaker, the deictic centre. Pronouns *I* and *you* are grounded in the point of view of the speaker: *I* refers to me when I say it, but to you when you say it. But that doesn't mean that first-person and second-person pronouns are always deictic: *you have to laugh or else you cry* is a generic usage.

English has a grammatical class of deixis signaled by word-initial voiced TH-: this one is better than *that* one. These are theirs. These words are known as function words – that is, words with little semantic content but which perform a grammatical function (voiceless TH -initial words (*think, thespian, thistle, thimble*) are not function words).

Note: There is a section on deixis in Jonathan Culpeper and Michael Haugh. 2014. *Pragmatics and the English Language*. Palgrave., and you might enjoy Massimiliano Morini. 2011. "Point of View in First-Person Narratives: A Deictic Analysis of David Copperfield." *Style*, 45/4, 598–618.

2 Demonstration of *deixis*

Here is a poem by Thom Gunn about his neighbours. See if you can spot deixis: remember, deictic expressions shift according to context and point to something outside the text.

'All Do Not All Things Well'

Implies that some therefore
Do well, for its own sake,
One thing they undertake,
Because it has enthralled them.

I used to like the two
Auto freaks as I called them
Who laboured in their driveway,
Its concrete black with oil,
In the next block that year.

One, hurt in jungle war,
Had a false leg, the other
Raised a huge beard above
A huge Hell's Angel belly.

They seemed to live on beer
And corn chips from the deli.

Always with friends, they sprawled
Beneath a ruined car
In that inert but live way
Of scrutinizing innards.
And one week they extracted
An engine to examine,
Transplant shining like tar
Fished out into the sun.

'It's all that I enjoy,'
Said the stiff-legged boy.
That was when the officious
Realtor had threatened them
For brashly operating
A business on the street
– An outsider, that woman
Who wanted them evicted,
Wanted the neighbourhood neat
To sell it. That was when

The boy from Viet Nam told me
That he'd firebomb her car.
He didn't of course, she won.

I am sorry that they went.
Quick with a friendly greeting,
They were gentle joky men
– Certainly not ambitious,
Perhaps not intelligent
Unless about a car,
Their work one thing they knew
They could for certain do
With a disinterest
And passionate expertise
To which they gave their best
Desires and energies.
Such oily-handed zest
By-passed the self like love.
I thought that they were good
For any neighbourhood.

Thom Gunn, 1992, *'All Do Not All Things Well'*

Here is the poem again, this time with the deixis marked in blue.

'All Do Not All Things Well'

Implies that some therefore
Do well, for its own sake,
One thing they undertake,
Because it has enthralled them.

I used to like the two
Auto freaks as I called them
Who laboured in their driveway,
Its concrete black with oil,
In the next block that year.

One, hurt in jungle war,
Had a false leg, the other
Raised a huge beard above
A huge Hell's Angel belly.

They seemed to live on beer
And corn chips from the deli.

Always with friends, they sprawled
Beneath a ruined car

In *that* inert but live way
Of scrutinizing innards.
And one week they extracted
An engine to examine,
Transplant shining like tar
Fished out into the sun.

'It's all that *I* enjoy,'
Said the stiff-legged boy.
That was when the officious
Realtor had threatened them
For brashly operating
A business on the street
– An outsider, *that woman*
Who wanted them evicted,
Wanted the neighbourhood neat
To sell it. *That* was when
The boy from Viet Nam told *me*
That he'd firebomb her car.
He didn't of course, she won.

I am sorry that they went.
Quick with a friendly greeting,
They were gentle joky men
– Certainly not ambitious,
Perhaps not intelligent
Unless about a car,
Their work one thing they knew
They could for certain do
With a disinterest
And passionate expertise
To which they gave their best
Desires and energies.
Such oily-handed zest
By-passed the self like love.
I thought that they were good
For any neighbourhood.

In the first stanza, I have not highlighted *some*, because it appears to refer anaphorically back to the *all* of the title (presumably with the head noun *people* elided).

There are several demonstratives in the poem:

> In the *next* block *that year*

The narrator's thoughts point to the block next to where he is, and to a specific year.

> In that inert but live way

This is known as empathetic deixis, the inert but live way being an abstract concept, conveying the narrator's view of the auto freaks' manner. It seems to be suggesting shared knowledge, but also distances (pointing to 'that way' rather than 'this way'), which is a characteristic of deixis.

> That was when the officious / Realtor had threatened them

The narrator's thoughts point to 'that time'.

> – An outsider, that woman / Who wanted them evicted

The narrator's thoughts point to *that woman – this woman* would work equally well semantically, meaning 'this woman whom I'm now discussing', but *that woman* keeps her at a distance. Deictic terms can be proximal (near to the speaker) or distal (distant from the speaker); *that woman* is distal.

> That was when / The boy from Viet Nam told me / That he'd firebomb her car.

The narrator's thoughts point to 'that time'.

In order to understand why the auto freaks are mending cars in a front yard rather than at a proper garage and why the realtor wants them gone, you need to know about veterans of the Vietnam War having trouble finding employment, and Hell's Angels looking intimidating. The poem is about people's judgement of appearances. Via the narrator, the deictic expressions link the auto freaks to the neighbourhood over time so as to make the auto freaks intrinsic to the neighbourhood. The narrator knows that the men are kind and gentle as he has observed them interacting over a period of several years. However, to the realtor, who does not know them, the men and their yard look filthy, intimidating, and smack of poverty. To her, appearances matter – she needs the place to look respectable in order to sell homes there. To the narrator, personal comportment and personal relationships are more important, and hence the distancing deixis.

3 Literary Exercise

Identify the deictic words in this poem. What does deixis do in this context?

Arrival at Santos

Here is a coast; here is a harbour;
here, after a meagre diet of horizon, is some scenery:
impractically shaped and – who knows? – self-pitying mountains,
sad and harsh beneath their frivolous greenery,

with a little church on top of one. And warehouses,
some of them painted a feeble pink, or blue,
and some tall, uncertain palms. Oh, tourist,
is this how this country is going to answer you

and your immodest demands for a different world,
and a better life, and complete comprehension
of both at last, and immediately,
after eighteen days of suspension?

Finish your breakfast. The tender is coming,
a strange and ancient craft, flying a strange and brilliant rag.
So that's the flag. I never saw it before.
I somehow never thought of there *being* a flag,

but of course there was, all along. And coins, I presume,
and paper money; they remain to be seen.
And gingerly now we climb down the ladder backward,
myself and a fellow passenger named Miss Breen,

descending into the midst of twenty-six freighters
waiting to be loaded with green coffee beans.
Please, boy, do be more careful with that boat hook!
Watch out! Oh! It has caught Miss Breen's

skirt! There! Miss Breen is about seventy,
a retired police lieutenant, six feet tall,
with beautiful bright blue eyes and a kind expression.
Her home, when she is at home, is Glens Fall

s, New York. There. We are settled.
The customs officials will speak English, we hope,
and leave us our bourbon and cigarettes.
Ports are necessities, like postage stamps, or soap,

but they seldom seem to care what impression they make,
or, like this, only attempt, since it does not matter,

the unassertive colours of soap, or postage stamps –
wasting away like the former, slipping the way the latter

do when we mail the letters we wrote on the boat,
either because the glue here is very inferior
or because of the heat. We leave Santos at once;
we are driving to the interior.

Elizabeth Bishop, 1952, *Arrival at Santos*

Here is the poem again, with the deictic expressions in blue:

Arrival at Santos

Here is a coast; here is a harbour;
here, after a meagre diet of horizon, is some scenery:
impractically shaped and – who knows? – self-pitying mountains,
sad and harsh beneath their frivolous greenery,

with a little church on top of one. And warehouses,
some of them painted a feeble pink, or blue,
and some tall, uncertain palms. Oh, tourist,
is this how this country is going to answer you

and your immodest demands for a different world,
and a better life, and complete comprehension
of both at last, and immediately,
after eighteen days of suspension?

Finish your breakfast. The tender is coming,
a strange and ancient craft, flying a strange and brilliant rag.
So that's the flag. I never saw it before.
I somehow never thought of there *being* a flag,

but of course there was, all along. And coins, I presume,
and paper money; they remain to be seen.
And gingerly now we climb down the ladder backward,
myself and a fellow passenger named Miss Breen,

descending into the midst of twenty-six freighters
waiting to be loaded with green coffee beans.
Please, boy, do be more careful with that boat hook!
Watch out! Oh! It has caught Miss Breen's

skirt! There! Miss Breen is about seventy,
a retired police lieutenant, six feet tall,
with beautiful bright blue eyes and a kind expression.
Her home, when she is at home, is Glens Fall

s, New York. There. We are settled.
The customs officials will speak English, we hope,
and leave us our bourbon and cigarettes.
Ports are necessities, like postage stamps, or soap,

but they seldom seem to care what impression they make,
or, like this, only attempt, since it does not matter,
the unassertive colours of soap, or postage stamps –
wasting away like the former, slipping the way the latter

do when we mail the letters we wrote on the boat,
either because the glue here is very inferior
or because of the heat. We leave Santos at once;
we are driving to the interior.

Analysis

In the second stanza, "And warehouses, / some of them painted a feeble pink, or blue", the quantifier *some* points to a subset of the warehouses which the narrator is observing. She is the deictic centre, singling out specific focal points for comment. *Oh, tourist*, is deictic if it directly addresses the narrator's companions, as is *after eighteen days* in the third stanza, if in reference to the specific eighteen days preceding the present, where the speaker is now; that is, the eighteen days spent sailing from home to Santos.

In the fourth stanza, "The tender is coming" *the* points to the tender belonging to the particular boat the narrator is on, just as when I say *the postman's late today*, I mean the postman who serves my house. *Coming* indicates motion towards the speaker's deictic centre. "So that's the flag" points to the flag of the country the narrator is about to enter, which she has just observed and identified. I have not marked *all along* in "I somehow never thought of there *being* a flag, / but of course there was, all along", as deictic, because the time-span refers anaphorically back (however vaguely) rather than extralinguistically. What about *Finish your breakfast?* Is this spoken by the poet to a companion, or by the ship's crew to the narrator?

In the fifth stanza, the narrator's reference to Miss Breen as a fellow passenger ("myself and a fellow passenger named Miss Breen") aligns Miss Breen with herself; the narrator is the deictic centre and Miss Breen is her fellow, included in the first-person plural pronoun of the eighth stanza ("There. We are settled."). However the tokens of *we* in the last stanza ("when we mail the letters we wrote on the boat,", "We leave Santos at once; / we are driving to the interior") point to all the people who (potentially) wrote letters on the boat, and any other disembarking tourists. The interior is deictic as from the point of view of Santos, it presumably refers to somewhere inland of São Paolo, but will shift its meaning each time the cruise-ship berths.

In the sixth stanza, the narrator addresses one of the crew as *boy*. *Boy* indicates the narrator's view of her social relationship to the referent, that is, as her social inferior, and either younger, or not younger but black. The crew, in her perception, are hired to serve the tourists.

There is much proximal deixis in this poem – the word *here* occurs four times, the pronoun *I/myself* four times, and the pronoun *we/us/our* nine times. The tokens of *there* are not distal; that is, they are not opposed to *here*. "I somehow never thought of there *being* a flag, / but of course there was, all along" has two tokens of *there*, but neither are deictic. They are both existential *there*, also known as dummy *there*. I have marked the token of *there* in "Watch out! Oh! It has caught Miss Breen's / skirt! There!" as deictic as I interpret it to mean that the boathook has ripped her skirt *there*, in that particular place, or *there*, just as the narrator predicted it would. I have marked the token of *there* in "There. We are settled" as deictic because it is an exclamation of completion, in this case, having negotiated the tricky transfer from ship to tender. There are two demonstratives: "that's the flag" and "that boat hook", both of which entities are proximal to the narrator.

Commentary

The poem is about the moment of disembarking at the port of Santos after an eighteen-day cruise at sea. Although Santos is not meant to be the focus of attention – the focus of attention is to be the interior – nevertheless the present moment in Santos astounds the narrator in various ways, from the frivolous greenery to the bleached buildings to the flag to the precarious descent down the ladder, and provokes her to feel insecure about all the things she does not know – the currency, the customs officials, their language, her allowance of alcohol and cigarettes, the glue on the postage stamps. Far from being a mere gateway to 'the interior', Santos presents the narrator with novel challenges of its own. The deixis of proximity serves to convey the immediacy of all these strange and new unknowns, and the narrator's resultant discomfiture and resolute resolve to meet them.

4 Teaching Point

Deixis is a useful concept for thinking about relationships; both relationships within the text, and authors' and readers' relationships to the text. Distal and proximal deixis in particular can be helpful concepts for literary analysis.

25 Conversational Implicatures

1 Definition of term *Conversational Implicatures*

Conversational Implicatures help with analysing the pragmatics of a conversation. Paul Grice (1975, *Logic and Conversation*) proposed four pragmatic maxims of Quantity, Quality, Relation and Manner. Grice's overall Co-operative Principle is: "A rough general principle which participants will be expected (*ceteris paribus* – other things being equal) to observe, namely: Make your conversational contribution such as is required, at the stage at which it occurs, by the accepted purpose or direction of the talk exchange in which you are engaged." (Grice 1975: 45). In other words, we converse co-operatively, and always try to understand each other in terms of exchanging information.

Maxims of Quantity

> Make your contribution to the conversation as informative as necessary.
>
> Do not make your contribution to the conversation more informative than necessary.

Consider the following short poem by Stevie Smith, where the damage is done in the last couplet by giving too much information:

> Come, wed me, Lady Singleton,
> And we will have a baby soon
> And we will live in Edmonton
> Where all the friendly people run.
>
> I could never make you happy, darling,
> Or give you the baby you want,
> I would always very much rather, dear,
> Live in a tent.
>
> I am not a cold woman, Henry,
> But I do not feel for you,
> What I feel for the elephants and the miasmas
> And the general view.
>
> Stevie Smith, 1942, *Lady 'Rogue' Singleton*

Maxims of Quality

Do not say what you believe to be false.

Do not say that for which you lack adequate evidence.

When someone says *you're a star*, this is not, on the surface, cooperative, as people are not stars but human beings. However by flouting the Maxim of Quality the implicature results that the co-locutor has star-like qualities (brightness, standing out). It is the implicature that maintains cooperation. Of course, if you deliberately lie, then you break the Maxims of Quality, and fail to maintain cooperation.

Maxim of Relation

Be relevant.

Otherwise you will confound, bore, mislead or perplex your listener. Children learn to observe the Maxim of Relation rather late on in childhood; ten-year-olds are still likely to announce whatever is on their mind rather than pertinent to the topic at hand.

Maxims of Manner

Avoid obscurity of expression.

Avoid ambiguity.

Be brief.

Be orderly.

References

Grice, Herbert P. 1975. Logic and Conversation. In Peter Cole & Jerry L. Morgan (eds.), *Syntax and Semantics*. Vol 3: *Speech Acts*, 41–58. New York: Academic Press.
See also Geoffrey N. Leech & Michael H. Short. 1981. *Style in Fiction*. London: Longman. (Chapter 9, especially section 9.1.2, pp. 294–9.)

2 Demonstration of term *Grice's Conversational Maxims*

Here is a very brief fictional conversation. As you read through, consider whether any of Grice's conversational maxims apply. Rosemary is Rhiannon's grown-up daughter.

When he had got out of his very shiny bright-blue car and at a second attempt shut its drivers's door, Malcolm revealed himself to be wearing a hacking jacket in dark red, green and fawn checks that were too large by an incredibly small amount, cavalry-twill trousers he must have been uncommonly fond of, a pale green I'm-going-out-for-the-day-with-my-old-girl-friend cravat or ascot and, thank goodness, a plain shirt and ordinary brown lace-up shoes. Seen closer to, he proved to have an ample shaving-cut on his cheek, about like a boil on the end of his nose to him and not worth a second glance to anybody else. He carried a florist's plastic-wrapped bouquet of a good forty-quid's-worth of red roses and pink carnations which he handed over to Rhiannon fast and at arm's length.

'Lovely to see you,' he muttered, obviously discarding on the spot an earlier draft, and called 'Hallo' with unmeant abruptness to Rosemary, whom he had met more than once before but never for long, and had not bargained on seeing now. Then he took in the puppy and loosened up a little. 'Ah, now here's a splendid fellow and no mistake.'

'Hallo, Malcolm,' said Rosemary, 'female fellow actually,' and went on with exemplary stuff about how he would not have said that if he had been on the spot just earlier, the awful chewing, etc. Rhiannon fixed the yellow rose in his button-hole and passed the bouquet to Rosemary, who had set Nelly down on the grass as now to be considered defused.

'Put them in that pretty Wedgwood jug – they'll look marvellous in there – and find somewhere in the cool for them.' Rhiannon was too shy herself to embark on a full-treatment head-on thank you. 'We'll decide on a proper place when I get back. That won't be before five at the earliest – I've got one or two things to see to in town first.' The last bit was said looking over her daughter's shoulder.

Kingsley Amis, 1986, *The Old Devils*

Fashion note: cravat or ascot?

Oxford English Dictionary cravat, *n.* 1. a. 'In modern use the term is usually applied either to a broad band of fabric (often colourful and highly patterned) worn around the outside of the collar, knotted or pinned in front, and typically forming part of a man's smart or formal outfit, or to a similar garment worn more casually, inside the collar of an open-necked shirt.'

Oxford English Dictionary Ascot, *n.*: 1957 M. B. Picken *Fashion Dict.* 10/1   Ascot. 1. Broad neckscarf, usually double. . . . 2. Double scarf that is informally looped under the chin.

Analysis

This conversation is not terribly successful as both Malcolm and Rhiannon are embarrassed. Malcolm has gone to great lengths over this visit: he's washed his car and put an abnormal amount of effort into his attire, choosing a jacket with a fussy design, trousers that anyone else would have got rid of and a pale green cravat or ascot. In the 1980s not many British men could carry off a pale green cravat or ascot successfully. And what about the clashing mixture of red roses and pink carnations, of which Malcolm has bought far too many? Presumably the opinions ("he must have been uncommonly fond of", "thank goodness", "exemplary") reflect Rhiannon's viewpoint – and her inability to tell the difference between cravats and ascots.

Malcolm flouts the Maxim of Quality in his hyperbolic expressions (*'lovely to see you,' 'splendid fellow', 'look marvelous'*), although such exaggeration is socially normal. It would be perverse to greet with 'you're looking relatively okay, given your age, income and genetic material, and your dog is dog-like', even though such observations would fulfill the Maxim of Quality. British social politeness convention demands that we say untruths in these situations, and to omit to do so gives offence. When Malcolm merely calls "Hallo" to Rosemary, without any further enquiry as to her health or comment on her well-being, he abides by the Maxim of Quantity, as he doesn't actually need this information. However he goes against politeness convention, which demands at least a minimal *How are you?*

Malcolm fails to perform *phaetic communication*, as does Rhiannon. *Phaetic communication* is the technical term for small-talk. *Small-talk* is a misnomer in that it sounds trivial whereas it is compulsory. People who manage phaetic communication well are thought to be charming; people who mismanage it give offence. Here, it is the emotionally-uninvolved Rosemary who is able to communicate phaetically, talking about the behaviour of the dog. What she says is unimportant semantically (*'exemplary stuff, the awful chewing, etc.'*) but important pragmatically. Knowing how to greet, how to say goodbye, when to keep silent, when to laugh, when to make eye-contact and how much, how to nod and make suitable facial expressions and look interested in your co-locutor – all of these vary from culture to culture, and are essential for successful communication. Typically, such skills are learnt relatively late in development. Teenagers can be judged surly when they haven't yet completed their repertoire of phaetic communication strategies.

Commentary

What did Malcolm and Rhiannon do wrong? Malcolm says '*Lovely to see you*', which is perfectly adequate and indeed better than the prepared speech would have been, but thrusts the expensive bouquet at arm's length without a comment, a compliment, or any kind of gesture of embrace or kiss on the cheek. He is also brusque with Rosemary. Rhiannon spends more time talking to, and embracing, Rosemary than she does Malcolm.

3 Literary Exercise

In the following text, Emm is Joy's aunt, and Joy and Tom are toddler Jonny's parents. Tom is just out of prison. How do Grice's maxims help explain how the utterances relate to each other?

Emm picks up her false teeth off the draining board and sticks them in her mouth.
　'I owe my tallyman fourteen pound. Mind you I had a pair of black tights and they've all shrivelled up, gone all funny.'
　There was a loud banging on the door. 'Three knocks Emm, that's us.'
　'This time of morning. You go Joy.'
　'Frit the blacks out of me that did.'
　Jonny ran to the door and Joy picked him up and carried him downstairs. She unlatched the door. There on the step stood Tom.
　'You've lost weight,' she said. 'I thought you weren't coming out till tomorrer.'
　'No today, trust you to get it wrong. Well aren't you going to let me in?'
　'I don't know as I should seeing as there's a divorce proceeding.'
　'Let me come in Joy – I want to see Jonny.' Jonny was hiding his face in his mother's neck. She led the way up the stairs.
　'Emm it's him – I've said he can have some tea.' On the landing mad Bet shrieked, 'Men, men, men, always men in there.'
　Tom sat on a chair, his face was blotchy from prison, his hands coarsened.
　Joy curled her pony tail round her fingers.
　'So what do you want?' Jonny still clung to her.
　'Hasn't he come on lovely Joy.'

'You make the tea,' said Emm. 'I'm going across for a packet of fags.'
'I met this bloke inside, given me the address of a place out at Catford. Two bedrooms, kitchen and balcony – only three quid a week and in perfect nick.'
'So?'
'Come back with me – give it a try for little Jonny's sake – I'll never lift a finger to you I promise.'
She stood apart from him and watched the tears run down his ugly face.
'I love you Joy.'
'I've got a lot to give up,' thought Joy. She looked round the room. 'At the same time I haven't got a lot to give up.'

Nell Dunn, 1967, *Poor Cow*

Analysis

Emm begins by commenting on her financial state (a *tallyman* supplied goods on credit, paid for in instalments), when she and Joy hear their specific door-knock signal of three knocks. *'Three knocks Emm, that's us.'*, says Joy, fulfilling all four maxims. *'This time of morning. You go Joy.'* replies Emm, fulfilling the Maxim of Relation by means of implicature. The knocks have nothing to do with the time of day in themselves; the implication is that Emm is not expecting visitors and resents the intrusion. Joy recognizes that this maxim has been fulfilled by picking up the affront and expanding on the unexpectedness of the knock: *'Frit the blacks out of me that did.'*

On seeing Tom, Joy says *'You've lost weight,'* and *'I thought you weren't coming out till tomorrer.'* Both of these observations fulfill the Maxim of Quality in that they are (presumably) true. Joy fulfills the Maxim of Relevance by implicature: her observation about his weight is due to his time in prison, and her statement about the date explains why she wasn't expecting him. Politeness convention demands a greeting when meeting one's spouse after a long absence, and Joy fails to give one. Tom cannot help but deduce that he is not particularly welcome.

Tom corrects her statement about the date: *'No today, trust you to get it wrong'* and asks: *'Well aren't you going to let me in?'* Joy responds negatively and gives her reason. He pleads, saying he wants to see his son, and she relents. Joy's comment to Emm *'Emm it's him – I've said he can have some tea.'*, fulfils the Maxim of Relation by implicature, as there is only one person sufficiently significant to be referred to as *him*.

Joy asks *'So what do you want?'*, challenging Tom to fulfil the Maxim of Relation ("be relevant"). As Joy has started to divorce Tom, his presence in her home cannot be taken for granted and he has to negotiate for it (at this point tactful Emm finds an excuse to remove herself: *'I'm going across for a packet of fags'*, the preposition *across* fulfilling the Maxim of Relation by implicature, meaning 'across the road').

Tom then gives information about the flat at Catford, which adheres to the Maxim of Relation by implicature, the implication being that he wants Joy to come and live with him there. She pretends to misunderstand by assuming that this maxim has been flouted and responds "*So*?". Tom then gives three other reasons. Joy has a conflicting response, thinking firstly of her independence, and then of her economic situation.

Commentary

Despite Joy's lack of cooperation, the conversation turns out to have been successful, as after the last sentence comes a blank line and three asterisks, indicating a minor pause in the chapter, and the subsequent paragraph begins "The flat out at Catford wasn't too bad".

4 Teaching Point

Grice's maxims are not necessarily adhered to on the surface; it is often the implicatures that enable cooperative conversation. British culture has a politeness code, which often causes problems for second-language learners. '*So what do you want?*', although direct and purposeful, is likely to give offence, as only in very close relationships can one be so direct.

26 Speech Acts

1 Definition of term *Speech Acts*

The concept of Speech Acts was first developed by J. L. Austin (*How To Do Things With Words*, 1962) and elaborated by John Searle (*Speech Acts*, 1969). When we talk, we do such things as greet, promise, warn, order, invite, congratulate, advise, thank, insult, and these are known as speech acts. From a literature student's point of view, Speech Act Theory can be a useful tool for those literary conversations where characters appear to be saying one thing but are really saying another, such as when a character is ostensibly giving advice but is actually delivering a threat; or when a character is ostensibly guiding tourists but is actually flirting. Doing two things at once when speaking is normal, of course; there's nothing especially literary about it.

An *illocutionary* act is one of asserting, demanding, promising, suggesting, exclaiming, vowing – anything that you can plausibly put the pronoun *I* in front of (*I warn you, I urge you, I thank you*). Illocutionary acts are declarations of personal view or intent. They are pronouncements from the self to the world. *Go!* ('I order you to go'); *I give thee my troth* (I am in the process of marrying you); *knit one, purl one* ('I order you to knit one, purl one). Illocutionary acts don't have to have an immediate, present, audience: *This is my last will and testament. This book belongs to Joe Bloggs.*

A *perlocutionary* act is one of getting somebody to do something; persuading (them to do something), convincing (them to think something), scaring (getting them to be afraid), insulting (getting them to be offended), amusing (getting them to laugh). Perlocutionary acts have an agenda, an agenda directed at someone else. They cannot take the pronoun *I* so easily: contrast *I urge you* with *I persuade you; *I advise you* with *I convince you.

2 Demonstration of *Speech Acts* in action

Here is an extract from a novel set in Ireland amongst the Anglo-Irish classes:

Sylvia was happily of her age and time. Competent, not wild. Pretty in the right and accepted way. Nothing embarrassingly clever about her. Everything she had was buttoned up and put away in little boxes. She was strong. Two of her girl friends arrived. They came on bicycles and leant their bicycles against the pillars of the portico and came into the cool hall with their rackets in their hands.

"Hallo, Sylvia."
"Hallo, Cecily, Hallo, Violet."
"Hallo, Sylvia."
"Lovely new balls."
"Who's coming?"
"Tony, Michael, Major Radley, John Wade, I think."
"How nice."
"What fun."
"I like your new blouse, Violet."
"I did all that faggot stitch myself."
"I hope there's coffee cake for tea."
"Yes, there is, greedy pig."
"Are they going to stay late?"
"Shall we dance?"
"We might. There's lots of cold food for supper."
"I want to play 'Whispering.'"
"'Whispering while you cuddle me near', oh, it's so lovely."
"'Whispering so no one near can hear me.'" They sang, wandering out of the house in their white shoes and stockings, carrying rackets and tennis balls to the smooth sunny grass where white painted seats were set in the wide fern-like shade of a cedar tree. There they waited for their men to arrive, pulling at their clothes and preening their hair like hen birds picking down the lengths of a breast-feather, answering each other absently, their minds put forward to the gay challenge of the hours to come.

Presently Grania came out and joined them. She was not fond of Sylvia's two girl friends. They played tennis too well and spoke to her almost kindly, but now she felt so grand and whole compared to them, half-living on kisses and glances and little no's that she was able to compete with them.

"How late your men are," she said, beginning with a wholesome broadside. She threw herself down on a rug, feeling the short grass with her hands.

"Just as well, dear," Sylvia said. "It will give you time to tuck your shirt inside your skirt, and even put on a pair of stockings without a hole in them. If you hurry."

"Oh, I can't really go to all that bother for a few men." Grania lay closer to the ground. "Though I admire you girls a lot for the trouble you take about yourselves."

"How are your other backhand shots getting on?" one of the friends asked.

"Oh, not bad at all."

"Don't underrate yourself, dear, you broke the drawing-room window so cleverly yesterday – one of your best strokes."

Grania giggled. Sylvia couldn't upset her.

M. J. Farrell (Molly Keane), 1941, *Two Days in Aragon*

Whispering

> Honey I have something to tell you,
> And it's worthwhile listening to;
> Put your little head on my shoulder,
> So that I can whisper to you:
> Whispering while you cuddle near me,
> Whispering so no one near can hear me,
> Each little whisper seems to cheer me,
> I know it's true, there's no one, dear but you;
> You're whispering why you'll never leave me,
> Whispering why you'll never grieve me;
> Whisper and say that you believe me,
> Whispering that I love you.

Whispering, 1920, by John Schonberger and Vincent Rose (music), and Richard Coburn (lyrics)

We can date the age and time of this fictional conversation because the song lyrics are taken from a real song: *Whispering*, 1920, with words by lyricist 'Richard Coburn', pseudonym for Frank Reginald DeLong (although attributed in 1920 to Malvin Schonberger, his brother reattributed it later) and music by composers John Schonberger and Vincent Rose. Sylvia, Cecily and Violet are waiting for the "gay challenge" of young men to show up and partner them at tennis. In fact the occasion is grim rather than gay as the undercurrent is one of determination, if not desperation – the girls are in competition with each other for potential husbands. Although this is not made explicit we can deduce it from their preening, their lack of attention to each other ("answering each other absently"), and their bitchiness.

> "I like your new blouse, Violet."
> "I did all that faggot stitch myself."
> "I hope there's coffee cake for tea."
> "Yes, there is, greedy pig."

The four verbs have illocutionary force: *I like, I did, I hope, there is*. Do any of the utterances have perlocutionary force? Is 'I did all that faggot stitch myself' a boast, in which case it is meant to discomfort the co-locutor, or is it mere fact? Is 'greedy pig' said in a friendly bantering manner, or is it barbed? In real life, we don't always know for sure. When Grania joins the three girls we can be certain that there is a malicious undercurrent as they are said to speak to her 'almost kindly'. The perlocutionary force of ""Just as well, dear," . . . "It will give you time to tuck your shirt inside your skirt, and even put on a pair of stockings without a hole in them. If you hurry"", is: 'You look a mess'. The address-term *dear*, in context, is sarcastic. Grania reacts in kind: ""Oh, I can't really go to all that bother for a few men." [. . .] "Though I admire you girls a lot for the trouble you take about yourselves."" The perlocutionary force is: "I don't need to dress up to attract men as you do, as I already have a boyfriend", and "It takes you an enormous amount of effort to look the way you do, which you need to do because unlike me you haven't yet attracted a boyfriend". The girls understand the perlocutionary force and one ripostes: ""How are your other backhand shots getting on?", referencing Grania's backhand compliment, which was no compliment at all.

3 Literary Exercise

Here is a phone conversation from the days of fixed landlines. Identify any perlocutionary utterances – do they further the conversation?

Note: a collect call was routed through the operator, and the receiver had to agree to pay the charges. *Silas Marner* is the name of a character in the novel of the same name by George Eliot, 1861. He lived in a slum.

But on the seventh ring she answered the phone and the operator asked her to accept a collect call from Pamela. "Will you accept?" she said.
    "Yes, I will," my mother said.
    Why it was just as if I had been wandering some Yorkshire moors for many days, through gorse and snow and sleet, even though it was practically ninety degrees outside! "Ma!" I said.
    "Where are you?" she said.
    "I'm at a pay phone," I said, "in the middle of a store."
    "So you can't talk?" she said.
    "Not really," I hissed, blinking over at the man. Now that my eyes had adjusted, I saw what a mockery of humanity this guy was. Gaunt, dressed in overalls with a soiled bib, swollen nose, and greasy red-blond hair and beard – he was playing some type of board game, alone, and there was something vaguely familiar about him. "Are you at your father's?" she said.

"Near," I said.
"And how is he?" she said.
"Uh-huh," I said
"Deceased?" she said.
"Uh-huh," I said.
There was a pause. "But otherwise, are you having a good time?"
"I can't hear you very well," I said. "There's a fly in my ear."
"Do you want me to drive there?" she said. "If I can find a substitute to teach my classes?"
"No!" I said. "That would only make things worse." Much as I loved my mother, I knew that very quickly after I saw her I would revert to adolescent behavior, due to the fact that during my adolescence I had never rebelled, and some part of me was making up for that now.
"Are you depressed?" she said.
"A little," I said.
"Maybe you're getting your period," she said.
There was something strangely unsatisfying about the conversation. Maybe too much time had gone by since we had last spoken and she had changed. "Well, this isn't much of a conversation," she said. "I guess you can't talk."
"That's right," I said.
"Something remarkable has happened here," she said.
"What?" I said.
"One of my students put her blue jeans in the washing machine and when she opened it she discovered a British Revolutionary War uniform. It's in excellent condition, practically new, and we're going to take it to the costume and clothing department of the Metropolitan Museum."
"Aw, Ma," I said. "She probably had one lying around or made it."
"I don't think so," she said. It would be impossible to fake it; they can do tests to determine its age through the fabric."
"So what do you think happened?" I said.
"I believe the washing machine was temporarily attached to some conduit opening onto the past. Now somebody in the Revolutionary War has a pair of new Levi's."
"If only something like that would happen to me!" I said.
"I know," my mother said.
"I would give anything for just one experience like that. Or if aliens landed and took me in their spacecraft, and injected me with some painful substance and then deposited me on the highway!"

"Have you seen any spacecraft out there?" my mother said.
"No," I said.
"Why don't you and Abdhul go out at night and look?" she said.

"Mm," I said, keeping one eye on Silas Marner. He was really rank, too, just my luck. Didn't it offend him to live with his own odor, or did he enjoy it? It reminded me of a man I had once found through an ad in the local paper to type some of my essays and my thesis in college. He had smelled, too. Human beings were very odd, I had forgotten this after being away from them in the woods.

"You really should keep your eyes out," my mother said. "I was just reading, how recently the CIA captured an alien, and apparently he's escaped. I'd send you the clipping, if you had a mailing address."

"Does the alien – have a strong scent?" I said in a hiss.

"What are you saying?" my mother said. "Does somebody there smell?"

"Yes!" I said triumphantly. That was all the proof I needed just now that my mother and I were still attuned to one another.

Tama Janowicz, 1992, *The Male Cross-Dresser Support Group*

Analysis

The speaker can't speak openly because 'Silas Marner' will overhear. Therefore she uses indirect speech acts in the hope that her mother will grasp her intent. Her rejoinders "Uh-huh", "Uh-huh", "Mm", have perlocutionary force, which her mother interprets successfully, even if she does not fully understand.

Commentary

The exchanges about the Revolutionary War uniform and space aliens are not literal illocutionary acts, they are place-holders for the real conversation which cannot take place. Their perlocutionary force is "I want to talk to you", "Are you alright?" and "Yes, I am".

4 Teaching Point

Conversations in literature sometimes convey more than the participants purport to say, either to each other, or to the reader. Speech Act Theory can be useful for analysing conversations with multiple agendas.

Primary Sources

Amis, Kingsley. 1986 [1987]. *The Old Devils*, 111–113; 203–204. Harmondsworth: Penguin.
Auden, W. H. 1956 [1981]. *First Things First.* In W. H. Auden, *Collected Shorter Poems 1927–1957*, 281. London: Faber and Faber.
Betjeman, John. 1972 [2013]. *Thank God it's Sunday.* BBC Archive. BBC Television: DVD.
Bishop, Elizabeth. 1952 [2000]. *Arrival at Santos.* In *The Nation's Favourite Poems of Journeys*, 108–109. London: BBC Worldwide Ltd.
Brookner, Anita. 1986. *A Misalliance*, 33. London: Grafton Books.
Raymond Chandler. 1953 [2010]. *The Long Good-Bye*, 38–40. Harmondsworth: Penguin.
Churchill, Caryl. 1982. *Top Girls*, 58–59. In *Churchill Plays: Two*. London: Methuen.
Danticat, Edwidge. 2002 [2004]. *Seven.* In *The Dew Breaker*, 48–49. New York: Alfred A. Knopf.
Dryden, John. 1667. *Annus Mirabilis: The Year of Wonders*, verses 215–222. Early English Books Online: http://name.umdl.umich.edu/A36598.0001.001.
Duhig, Ian. 1991. *I'r Hen Iaith A'i Chaneuon.* In *The Bradford Count*, 33. Newcastle upon Tyne: Bloodaxe Books.
Dunn, Nell. 1967 [2013]. *Poor Cow*. 110–111. London: Virago.
Farrell, M. J. (Molly Keane). 1941 [1985]. *Two Days in Aragon*, 96–97. London: Virago Modern Classics.
Fitzgerald, F. Scott. 1925. *The Great Gatsby*, 39. New York: Charles Scribner's Sons.
Fitzgerald, Penelope. 1979. *Offshore*, 46–47. London: Magnum Books.
Fitzgerald, Zelda. 1932 [1993]. *Save Me the Waltz.* In Matthew J. Bruccoli (ed.), *The Collected Writings of Zelda Fitzgerald*, 171–172. London: Abacus Books.
Forster, E. M. 1905 [1985]. *Where Angels Fear to Tread*, 48–49. Edited by Oliver Stallybrass. Harmondsworth: Penguin.
Graham, Laurie. 1998. *The Dress Circle*, 46–47. London: Black Swan Books.
Green, Henry. 1950 [1992]. *Nothing*, 67–68. London: Harvill.
Greene, Graham. 1938 [1976]. *Brighton Rock*, 71–72. Harmondsworth: Penguin.
Gunn, Thom. 1992. *'All Do Not All Things Well'.* In *The Man with Night Sweats*, 52–53. London: Faber and Faber.
Heaney, Seamus. 1979. *Glanmore Sonnets*, VII. *Field Work*, 39. London: Faber and Faber.
Jacobs, A. C. 1976 [2004]. *N.W.2: Spring.* In Gerard Benson, Judith Chernaik & Cicely Herbert (eds.), *New Poems on the Underground*, 73. London: Cassell.
Janowicz, Tama. 1992. *The Male Cross-Dresser Support Group*, 202. New York: Crown Publishers.
Jerome, Jerome K. 1900 [1983]. *Three Men on the Bummel*, 143. Harmondsworth: Penguin.
Jesse, F. Tennyson. 1934. *A Pin to See the Peepshow*, 91. Harmondsworth: Penguin.
Joyce, James. 1922. *Ulysses*, 695. Paris: Shakespeare and Company.
Kerouak, Jack. 1957 [1991]. *On the Road*, 17-18. Harmondsworth: Penguin Classics.
Larkin, Philip. 1955 [1988]. *Mr Bleaney.* In Anthony Thwaite (ed.), *Philip Larkin Collected Poems*, 102–103. London: The Marvell Press and Faber and Faber.
Mamet, David. 1984 [1993]. *Glengarry Glen Ross*, 47–49. London: Methuen.
Morrison, Arthur. 1894. *Lizerunt.* In *Tales of Mean Streets*, 31–36. London: Methuen and Co.
Nash, Ogden. 1938 [2000]. *Columbus.* In *The Nation's Favourite Poems of Journeys*, 107. London: BBC Worldwide Ltd.
Okri, Ben. 1998 [1999]. *Infinite Riches*, 236–237. London: Orion.
Peake, Mervyn. 1959 [1998]. *Titus Alone*, 11–12. London: Vintage.
Pinter, Harold. 1981 [2005]. *Family Voices.* In Harold Pinter, *Plays 4*, 131–133. London: Faber and Faber.

Poultney, Clifford B. 1923. *Mrs. 'Arris*, 106. London: Herbert Jenkins.
Rhys, Jean. 1934 [1991]. *Voyage in the* Dark. In *The Early Novels*, 81. London: Andre Deutsch.
Robinson, Mary. 1800. *London's Summer Morning*. In *Whitehall Evening Post*, Issue 8281, 21 August 1800.
Sanchez, M. G. 2021 [2022]. *Marlboro Man*, 12-13. Gibraltar: The Dabuti Collective.
Selvon, Sam. 1956 [1999]. *The Lonely Londoners*, 92-93. Harlow: Longman/Pearson Education Limited.
Smith, Stevie. 1949 [1981]. *A London Suburb*. In Jack Barbera & William McBrien (eds.), *Me Again, Uncollected Writings of Stevie Smith*, 100. London: Virago Press.
Smith, Stevie. 1958 [1981]. *On the Dressing gown lent me by my Hostess the Brazilian Consul in Milan, 1958*. In Jack Barbera & William McBrien (eds.), *Me Again, Uncollected Writings of Stevie Smith*, 246-247. London: Virago Press.
Smith, Stevie. 1942 [1978]. *Lady 'Rogue' Singleton*. In James MacGibbon (ed.). *Stevie Smith Selected Poems*, 105. Harmondsworth: Penguin.
Spark, Muriel. 1960. *The Bachelors*, 70-72. London: Macmillan.
Swift, Graham. 1996. *Last Orders*, 1-3. London: Picador.
Taylor, Elizabeth. 1976 [2006]. *Blaming*, 78-79. London: Virago Modern Classics.
Thomas, Dylan. 1954 [1991]. *Under Milk Wood: A Play for Voices*, 11. London: J. M. Dent and Sons.
Tonouchi, Lee A. 2001. da mayor of lahaina. *Da Word. Bamboo Ridge. Journal of Hawai'i Literature and Arts* 78, 96-97. Honolulu: Bamboo Ridge Press.
Walcott, Derek. 1990. *Omeros*, 193-195. London: Faber and Faber.
Waugh, Evelyn. 1930 [1953]. *Vile Bodies*, 52. Harmondsworth: Penguin.
Welch, Denton. 1948 [1963]. *The Trout Stream*. In Jocelyn Brooke (ed.). *Denton Welch Extracts from his Published Works*, 108-109. London: Chapman and Hall Ltd.
Wells, H. G. 1911. *The New Machiavelli*, 66-67. London: John Lane The Bodley Head.
Winterson, Jeanette. 2004. *Lighthousekeeping*, 31. Oxford: Isis Publishing Ltd.
Woolf, Virginia. 1925 [1976]. *Mrs Dalloway*, 6. London: Granada.

References

Introduction

Cauldwell, R.T. (1994) 'Discourse Intonation and Recordings of Poetry: Philip Larkin Reads *Mr Bleaney*', unpublished doctoral dissertation, University of Birmingham.

Chapter 1

Stiubhart, Domhnall Uilleam. 2017. The Making of the Minch: French Pirates, British Herring, and Vernacular Knowledges at an Eighteenth-Century Maritime Crossroads. In David Worthington (ed.), *The New Coastal History: Cultural and Environmental Perspectives from Scotland and Beyond*, 131–148. Cham, Switzerland: Palgrave Macmillan.
Oxford English Dictionary: oed.com.

Chapter 19

Cooper, Brian. 2008. Contribution to the study of a euphemism in the intimate lexis of Slavonic and Germanic Languages. *Transactions of the Philological Society* 106/1. 71–91.
Geeraerts, Dirk. 2008. Prototypes, stereotypes and semantic norms. In Gitte Kristiansen & R. Dirven (eds.), *Cognitive Sociolinguistics: Language Variation, Cultural Models, Social Systems*, 21–44. Berlin/New York: Mouton de Gruyter.
Immonen, Visa. 2014. Fondling on the kitchen table – artefacts, sexualities and performative metaphors from the 15th to the 17th centuries. *Journal of Social Archaeology* 14/2. 177–195.
Wright, Laura. 2023. *The Social Life of Words*. Oxford: Blackwells.

Chapter 21

Wales, Katie. 2000 [1989]. *A Dictionary of Stylistics*. Harlow: Longman.

Chapter 23

Ivanchenko, Andriy. 2007. An 'interactive' approach to interpreting overlapping dialogue in Caryl Churchill's *Top Girls* (Act 1). *Language and Literature* 2007 16/1. 74–89.

Chapter 24

Culpeper, Jonathan & Michael Haugh. 2014. *Pragmatics and the English Language*. Basingstoke: Palgrave Macmillan.

Morini, Massimiliano. 2011. Point of View in First-Person Narratives: A Deictic Analysis of David Copperfield. *Style* 45/4. 598–618.

Chapter 25

Grice, Herbert P. 1975. Logic and Conversation. In Peter Cole & Jerry L. Morgan (eds.), *Syntax and Semantics*. Vol: *Speech Acts*, 41–58. New York: Academic Press.

Leech, Geoffrey N. & Michael H. Short. 2007 [1981]. *Style in Fiction: a Linguistic Introduction to English Fictional Prose*. Harlow: Pearson Longman.

Chapter 26

Austin, John L. 1962. *How To Do Things With Words*. Editedy by J. O. Urmson & Marina Sbisà. Oxford: Clarendon Press.

Searle, John. 1969. *Speech Acts*. Cambridge: Cambridge University Press.

www.ingramcontent.com/pod-product-compliance
Lightning Source LLC
Chambersburg PA
CBHW051523230426
43668CB00012B/1714